George W. Westphal

Ephraim

Wis

# LETTERS OF
# PRINCIPAL JAMES DENNEY

Photo T & R Annan & Sons, Glasgow.

Ever yours sincerely
James Denney

# LETTERS OF
# PRINCIPAL JAMES DENNEY

## TO

## W. ROBERTSON NICOLL

## 1893-1917

HODDER AND STOUGHTON LIMITED

LONDON    NEW YORK    TORONTO

# CONTENTS

# PREFATORY NOTE

THIS volume is not a biography of Principal
Denney. The field for that is still clear, and it is
to be hoped that it will be occupied. In the
meantime, and with the cordial concurrence of
his immediate relatives, I have ventured to put
together the following selection from his letters
to me during an intimate friendship which lasted
over a quarter of a century.

Our intercourse began when I invited him to
contribute translations to the *Foreign Biblical
Library*. Afterwards it made great progress.
Principal Denney wrote commentaries in the
*Expositor's Bible* and in the *Expositor's Greek
Testament*. We discussed together his other
books. He agreed to furnish regular contributions
to the *British Weekly* which I edited. These
were often leading articles, and many of them
were signed. Every week almost he sent me
some reviews of new books, and their remarkable
qualities of incisiveness and scholarship attracted
attention and admiration. In sending his contributions he was very often good enough to enclose

a letter, and it is from these letters that I have made up this book. It will be seen that they deal with most of the controversies which disturbed the world during these years. We were not always of the same mind, but we never differed in sympathy. The subjects touched upon in this correspondence are such as the Atonement; the situation created by the action of the House of Lords in the case of the United Free Church of Scotland; the unsuccessful attempt made to establish a magazine for the united Church; the proposals of the Church of Scotland for Presbyterian union; Social Reform; Local Option and State Purchase; and, above all, the war. I have not kept more than a fraction of his letters, but I trust that what remains will be found stimulating and characteristic. Very few omissions have been made from the letters. There was never any venom in Dr. Denney's pen, but he was both keen and frank as a critic. In the Appreciation I have partially reproduced an article I wrote on his death, and have strengthened it with quotations from the tribute paid by his colleague Professor James Moffatt in the *British Weekly*. I acknowledge with much gratitude the contribution made to this book by one of Dr. Denney's most distinguished students, Professor J. A. Robertson, of Aberdeen. I am deeply indebted to Dr. Denney's intimate friend, the Rev. W. R. Thomson, of Bellshill, for a very suggestive letter, and I thankfully acknowledge the help received from my colleagues Miss Jane Stoddart and Sir Ernest Hodder-Williams; also from the volume of the Rev. T. H. Walker.

HAMPSTEAD, *October* 1920.

# APPRECIATION

## By W. ROBERTSON NICOLL

# APPRECIATION

JAMES DENNEY was born at Paisley on February 5, 1856. He was educated at first at the Highlanders' Academy in Greenock, a large school providing a thoroughly sound but plain education at a low charge. The headmaster in Denney's time was Mr. William Bowie, a robust, red-haired resourceful man of middle age. He maintained strict discipline and he was a born teacher. James Denney became a pupil teacher, and was from the first very successful with the boys. He was tall and slight, with a grave yet kindly expression, the student and scholar written in every line of his face. A startling contrast to Denney in that old Academy was found in John Davidson, the poet, who was a scholar and teacher at the same time. Davidson was the son of an Evangelical Union minister, and I remember a conversation in which he told me that his father was a man of rare ability.

From school Mr. Denney passed to the University of Glasgow. He matriculated as an Arts student in November 1874, and took an eminent position from the first. One of his

colleagues, Dr. Clow, says that in the Latin
Class a stillness at once fell upon the students
as, in level tones and with perfect enunciation,
the listeners heard a translation as loyal to the
original as it was clean-edged and felicitous.

Mr. Denney was fortunate in his professors.
He won Edward Caird's coveted Gold Medal.
But he never accepted Caird's philosophy, and
though learned in the history of philosophy he
declined to tie himself to any system, holding
that one system gave way to another and that
Christianity was bound up with none of them.
His unreserved admiration was given to Professor
Jebb. To the biography of Professor Jebb
Dr. Denney contributed an appreciation. He
admitted that Jebb could not in any sense
fraternise with his pupils, the main interest of
most of them being too remote from his own,
yet he was most willing to help those who sought
his guidance in his own field. ' What impressed
the imperfectly prepared students, who had to
do any work for Mr. Jebb, was the precision and
finish of all his work for them. Most of us had
no idea of what translation could be—whether
from Greek into English or from English into
Greek. His renderings of Sophocles, which have
since become known to all the world, came on
us like a revelation. He not only did the thing,
but created an ideal for us by doing it.' Denney,
after leaving the University, assisted Jebb for

some years in examination work, and was impressed by the interest that the Cambridge scholar took in the progress of his men.

Another professor with whom he came to work was Professor Veitch, of the Logic Class. Denney assisted him. A pupil at that time says : ' What drew one's attention to this man with the slender frame, the scholar's stoop, the countenance " sicklied o'er with the pale cast of thought," the intent look, the reticent manner, the metallic tone of speech, was his character rather than his career in Arts, brilliant as that had been.'

James Denney's parents belonged to the Reformed Presbyterian Church. The little denominations in Scotland have been fruitful in giving us great Christian leaders. Denney passed over to the Free Church, taking with him his stern but warm piety, his appreciation of dogmatic truth, and his hearty interest in the Church of Christ. He proceeded in time to the Free Church College, Glasgow, where students were under the stimulating influence of A. B. Bruce, J. S. Candlish, and T. M. Lindsay. Perhaps it was Bruce who most influenced Denney. Denney admired his work, and especially his Commentary on the Synoptic Gospels. Denney had a period of what might be called Broad Churchism, but when Bruce and his pupil came to the fork in the road the master took one way and the scholar another. He was reticent in describing his spiritual history, but I believe that his wife, who gave him the truest and most perfect companionship, led him into a more pronounced evangelical creed. It was she who induced him to read Spurgeon, whom he had been inclined to despise. He became an ardent admirer of the preacher and a very careful and sympathetic student of his sermons. It was Spurgeon perhaps as much as any one who led him to the great decision of his life— the decision to preach the Atoning Death of the Lord Jesus Christ. This, as Dr. Moffatt has said, was all in all to him. He spent and was spent in making it everything to the Church.

He went first, in 1886, to Broughty Ferry as minister of the East Free Church. There he wrote his Commentaries on the Epistles to the Thessalonians and the Second Epistle to the Corinthians, in the *Expositor's Bible*. His relations with the Church were so intimate through all changes that one of his successors generously declared that he was minister of the East Church till the day of his death. In one of his sermons he states his position with the utmost clearness :—

' In one way of it the Christian life always begins with a great humiliation. Christ comes to us as One without Whom we cannot take the first step in the new way of life ; even to begin it we must be infinitely and for ever indebted to Him.   How do we need to begin ?   All we sinful men need to begin with the forgiveness of sins.   Now when we think of it, when we think of the forgiveness of sins, what are we to say ?   We cannot earn it, we cannot claim it, we cannot take it for granted, we must go into debt for it, and we must go into debt to Christ. That is the very heart of the Gospel.   Christ brings the forgiveness of sins, and He brings it at an unspeakable cost.   Christ died for the ungodly :   " in Whom we have redemption through His blood, even the forgiveness of our trespasses, according to the riches of His grace." '

He also delivered in America, and published in 1895, his memorable *Studies in Theology*. There followed his precious Commentary on the Epistle to the Romans in the *Expositor's Greek Testament*—perhaps the very best piece of work he ever accomplished—and his weighty volumes, *The Death of Christ* and *Jesus and the Gospel*. His book of sermons, *The Way Everlasting*, presents his characteristic thoughts with marked simplicity and power, and has taught many ministers how the Cross of our Lord Jesus Christ may be preached.

He was very happy as a pastor, but he found his true place and legitimate sphere when he was appointed a Professor in the United Free

Church College, Glasgow. This was in 1897.
He was eminently fortunate in his surroundings.
No Divinity School of the world stood higher.
He had the warmest appreciation of his colleagues, and it was fully returned. The scholarly,
laborious, and courageous Professor Orr was a
close friend. The learned and accomplished
Principal, Dr. T. M. Lindsay, had a very special
place in his regard. Professor George Adam
Smith brought with him ' an intellectual and
moral stimulus of which he would speak sometimes with a singular note of intensity.' With
the students he was eminently successful. He
had all the qualities needed for a great religious teacher—profound piety, wide culture, and
scholarship which could not be gainsaid. It has
been well said that he was a living conscience
among his men. A favourite phrase of their
professor was ' Crowd in conscience.' And this
he did himself, for even more prominent than
his teaching was the high standard of duty and
responsibility he set up for those who would
be ministers of Jesus Christ. It is not easy to
induce theological students to be students in
earnest. But Denney could not endure a shirker,
and though he did not storm he could speak
in a stern, quiet way when anything displeased
him. Some of the students were in awe of him,
but his rich, generous personality conquered all.
His genial sympathies, his catholic taste in

literature, proved the breadth of his nature. Dr. Moffatt has told us of his intimate knowledge of the eighteenth century. His lectures on Johnson, Gibbon, and Burns were monographs of a high order. He said to a friend that if the historical plays of Shakespeare were lost he could reproduce them from memory. He could find a place for Byron. When a friend argued that you must be under twenty to get a real taste of Byron, ' Yes,' he said quickly, ' but Byron has something for us even in the sixties '— though he humorously refused to disclose what it was. He indulged himself in light reading, and shortly before his death he was especially caught by ' Q.'s ' fiction, reading with delight *Troy Town* and *The Delectable Duchy*. Graver studies went along with these, and he would speak of what he had found in St. Bernard, and of how much he had been disappointed in Aquinas and the Puritans.

I have a certain mournful pride in thinking that I did something to induce him to come forward as an author. At that time his mind was fully made up, his future was foreseen, he was to preach the Cross of Christ—on the one hand its power to save, and on the other its sharpness and sternness, its imperious calls to duty and self-denial. From this preaching of the Cross he was never moved, but as time went on he became more and more master of a style

which did justice to the great thoughts. In
fact, his *Studies in Theology* are perhaps the
freshest and brightest of his writings. It was
his deep conviction that want of style prevented
almost all Scottish theological books from reach-
ing the first rank. Indeed, he held that Macleod
Campbell's treatise on the Atonement was the
only classical theological book that came from
Scotland. Like Dale he drilled himself in Burke.
There was much in Denney that recalled Dale,
and the older man recognised with joy a true
fellow soldier. I do not say that Dr. Denney
rose into poetry or that his imagination was
highly developed. His wife used to say laugh-
ingly that there was not enough pathos in his
sermons. There was, however, a deep evangelical warmth and tone. He learned to write
with self-command, a majestic sense of simplicity and precision, a deliberate measure of
expression, a resolute limitation of general statements by the severity of facts. This serious
clearness, this grasp of his own thoughts, is
most plainly seen in his chief book, *Jesus and
the Gospel.* What was said of a great preacher
may be said about Dr. Denney. His inmost
spirit was busy with the New Testament. He
preached New Testament doctrines as one who
lived in the presence of great subjects, subduing
him, restraining him, calling for self-recollection
and sober words. By dint of constant labour

he arrived at a style which was the perfection
of lucidity.

Dr. Denney loved controversy, and he was
one of the most formidable of fighters. It is
needless to say that he scorned personal disputes and took no part in them. But he had
a profound contempt for sciolism. He was completely armed, a thorough scholar, in full command of all his weapons, with these weapons
always at their brightest. A keen logician, he
could detect and expose a fallacy with almost
supernatural quickness. He had great powers
of irony and sarcasm, but he was incapable of
striking a foul blow. His insight was hardly
ever at fault, and he could take the measure of
disputants. Dr. Denney was one of the most
modest of men, simple to a degree in his manner,
absolutely free from pretentiousness of any kind.
Sometimes he appeared to be aloof. Many men
feared him. But his nature was gentle. He
could think and speak with a readiness and
clearness and keenness to which few could
attain. For years he wrote none of his sermons,
but one might listen to him and fail to find a
sentence unfinished or a wrong word used. It
was in this way that he came to be the power he
was. In any assembly that might be gathered
he was, when he chose, the leader. Scotland,
happily, is still very rich in great preachers and
scholars and theologians, but I think they will

be the foremost to admit that none of them is quite on the same level as the master we mourn. One of the most eminent leaders of the Church of Scotland was known to say that the whole decision with regard to Union lay with Dr. Denney. If he supported Union it would carry. If he opposed it, it could not be carried.

His chief sorrow was the death of his wife, which took place some years before his own. This made a great difference to Dr. Denney, but the subject is too sacred to be written of. Whatever he did was strengthened and completed by her constant watchfulness and aid, and I have often thought that her death gave him a better comprehension of the deeper problems and tragedies of the heart. Not that he was unsympathetic. He was the most sympathetic of men, but he had much of the Scottish reticence, and he did not wear his heart on his sleeve.

An impressive testimony to the growing esteem in which he was held was given by his appointment, in 1914, to succeed Principal T. M. Lindsay, who for forty years was identified with the Glasgow College. When the General Assembly met in 1915, it was found that the Church was united as to this appointment. Denney's name was the only one mentioned. After his nomination had been proposed and seconded, the whole Assembly rose to its feet

when the newly elected Principal was introduced
to the House, escorted by his proposer and
seconder. It was a magnificent and moving
spectacle, which was only intensified by the
humble bearing of the man on whom was con-
ferred this spontaneous tribute. In a few brief
sentences he declared his willingness to accept
the appointment, making the characteristic remark that the chief joy of such things is the
demonstration they give of the amount of good-
will there is in the world. Dr. Moffatt has told
us that what he said in his college, what he was,
mattered as little else did.

So the years went on, crowded with labours.
A warning came when he was attacked by
illness, and was confined for some months to his
room. He was allowed to see very few friends,
but he had his books, and it was hoped that
six months of total rest might restore him.
He was only sixty-one—comparatively young
as years are counted now.

He was taken away at a time when he had
reached the highest point of his influence. He
would have gone much higher if he had been
spared to us, through the sheer strength and
beauty and wisdom of his nature. He never
sought power. He was one of the most un-
worldly, unselfish, retiring of men, and was in a
manner forced to the front. In his own Church,
the United Free Church, he was the chief leader.

In his beloved city of Glasgow he had come to
be one of the most influential of public men.
All over the world he had his readers and
followers. That he was in many respects the
first man in Scotland was coming to be acknowledged. It is my own deliberate opinion that
hardly any greater loss could have befallen
the Christian Church, for he seemed destined to
guide thought and action in the difficult years
to come as hardly any one could but himself.

There is no doubt that he sacrificed himself.
The zeal of God's house had eaten him up.
Not content with his work as student, professor,
and author, he undertook the charge of the
Central Fund of his Church, moved by a deep
sympathy with the needs of his brethren, and
to that noble cause he gave himself continually.
He was also preparing to deliver the Cunningham
Lectures, and had chosen for his subject the
Atonement. He preached incessantly, generally
twice every Sunday. Also he had been called
to leadership in great vital causes. His whole
soul was absorbed in the movement for Prohibition and in the resistance of State Purchase.
He slipped almost insensibly into a large share
of ecclesiastical work. His pen was always
ready. He gave us in the *British Weekly* such
help as no other man could, and over a period of
many years I never remember him refusing any
request. Thus he was continually spending

himself, and all of us seemed to take it for granted that he was capable of any labour. Also he thought so himself. But, alas! we were all wrong.

It is a hard task in writing of a friend who has gone to analyse and reproduce for others, as a picture, that of which we feel the reality and perhaps do not care to feel more. Yet something must be said somehow. To me he was the truest, the warmest, and the tenderest of friends. Our intimate association lasted unclouded for more than twenty-five years. From his sick chamber he found time to write to me. I take leave to print a few lines from this letter :—

' I am counting on the open air, which I have not breathed for seven weeks or so, to set me up again. I don't know what was wrong with me : I just collapsed suddenly and completely like the one hoss shay in O. W. Holmes, and I have spent all these weeks in painfully gathering myself in bits out of the *débris*. I am past the point of despair now, but when I shall be able to do any kind of work with body or brain I cannot foresee. I have been a little astonished at the people who condoled with me on having to postpone the Cunningham Lectures : the things I am sore at being unable to help are the Temperance cause and the Central Fund.'

What we have lost in him we shall have to discover in travelling what remains of the journey. We cannot realise that this eager tenderness, this high, self-possessed and furnished intellect should have been taken from us. Everything reminds us that at a moment when we most needed such a mind we must look for it no more.

Dr. Moffatt recalls what Denney once said about one of his favourites, Dr. Johnson. The two were speaking of Boswell's paragraphs at the end, and he remarked, ' The best thing said about Johnson's loss was not said by Boswell.' When asked what he meant he quoted Gerard Hamilton's words : ' Johnson is dead. Let us go to the next best—there is nobody ; no man can be said to put you in mind of Johnson.'

' To the last he was able usually to work. His Greek Testament and notebooks were beside his bed when I last saw him, and he was planning new lectures, talking of theology, of Professor Gwatkin's library, of Tertullian, even as he gasped for breath.'

But it is all in vain that we try to tell how much we miss him. Francis Thompson wrote :—

> ' When a grown woman dies,
>     You know we think unceasingly
>   What things she said, how sweet, how wise,
>     And these do make our misery.'

It is not with mere misery that we think of Dr. Denney. We are happy in the remembrance of a man in whose presence we felt that God and goodness could not be doubted. But the

news of his death was a blow on the heart.
' Alas ! my brother, very pleasant wast thou
unto me.'

I recall Dean Church's words about Hugh
James Rose. ' As far as could be seen at the
time, he was the most accomplished divine
and teacher in the English Church. He was
a really learned man. He had the intellect and
energy and literary skill to use his learning.
He was a man of singularly elevated and religious
character ; he had something of the eye and
temper of a statesman, and he had already
a high position. He was profoundly loyal to
the Church, and keenly interested in whatever
affected its condition and its fortunes.'

# MEMORIES OF A STUDENT

By the Rev.

Professor J. A. ROBERTSON, M.A., Aberdeen

# MEMORIES OF A STUDENT

WHEN Dr. Denney appeared one day as preacher at King's College Chapel, Old Aberdeen, two youths went to hear him, with anticipations whetted; and the first impression was one of disappointment. There was nothing prophetic, or even leonine, about the physical build of this reputed defender of the Faith. His longish face, with the dark, close-cropped hair and beard, had the pallor of the student about it. And when he began to speak, his thin, high-pitched voice was not immediately magnetic. But his language had an athletic and purposive directness. It knew where it was going, and made straight for the mark, taking every obstacle on the way with the ease which only comes with long discipline in thinking. He had not been speaking long before we detected that the clear note of the voice had in it the ring and clash as of a bright, well-tempered sword. The *riposte* was perfect—without any fumbling or faltering. 'It is frequently said that Christianity is on its trial to-day. That is precisely what it is in the nature of Christianity to be. It is a thing that is *always* on its trial in the world.'

And one felt that he himself was an embodiment of the truth he spoke : a trained swordsman, always on guard, always ready to do battle for the cause that was his very life's-blood. The incisive mind gripped and held : and a disciple was won that day.

When I went to Glasgow to study under him, the old spell was at once laid on the mind by Denney the teacher. At first we reacted against it somewhat. The minds of the class were but half-disciplined, and eager with a half-informed passion for liberty of thought, which was really, I suppose, licence. We hardly knew then that liberty had its perfect law, in the world of thought as elsewhere. In the minds of most of us there was a smattering of the elusive idealism current in the universities. And we felt the pull of a mind strenuously shepherding us into a pathway which seemed to us somewhat hedged in, and which for him was the only pathway leading to ' reality,' his favourite, or most characteristic word. How often was theory or opinion tossed aside with intellectual indignation as ' unreal to the last degree,' or some such word.

The qualities of his mind which impressed us were a precision and exactness of scholarship which could not tolerate looseness or short-cuts or slovenliness ; a limpid clarity which glittered like a mountain stream with a kind of fierce

impatience of all tangled and confused thinking ; a sincerity, a feeling for truth, which was
ever scornful of mere futility or irrelevance or
trifling finesse ; and a passionate intensity which
was contemptuous of superficiality or vague
imaginative sentiment.

The high, close-packed, shining temples, the
thin, mobile lips that never moved to utterance
but with the considered and significant word,
the speculative, almost Jewish, nose, the dark,
piercing eyes behind the close-poised spectacles,
the pallor of the face—all became transfigured
for us. They were symbolic of so much more
than the merely studious mind : symbolic of an
intellectual asceticism which had no use for the
beauty that was not also purposive, the emotion
which was not moral, or the fine which was not
also the true. Not—as I have said—that he
was not passionate : ' passionate scholarship '
is a phrase which describes his work as well as
any. But all his passions seemed to be called
off from the pursuit of other ends in life, and
dedicated wholly to the service of the mind and
conscience, which in their turn were dedicated
wholly to his Master.

It was an exhilarating experience to watch
his relentless and inexorable logic remorselessly
pursuing some theory : probing, *e.g.*, that persistent tendency of the Teutonic mind to find
some hidden motive behind the artless naïveté

of an evangelist's words ; then finally, with one last, pitiless thrust, leaving the man with his theory, wriggling, a mere worm in the dust, while the class gasped at the deftness of the knock-out blow : ' And so this evangelist has gone on deceiving the world all these centuries— *till Schmiedel found him out !* '

Behind it all one recognised the presence of a profound and definite spiritual experience which he himself had lived through.  You often hear men say of such a man : ' His life has been hedged-in from the tragedy of the world ; he has not felt, and has no sympathy with the struggles and temptations of ordinary men.'  It is simply not true of Denney.  His teaching had the note of battle about it, because he himself had fought, and was ever fighting, for the faith that was in him.  He did experience the struggles of other men, though his spoken word was never introspective ; but to this battle, which lies in the life of every man, there was added the battle of a man who had been brought up in a strict orthodoxy of religious outlook, the spirit of which he had made his own in his loyalty to truth, and the rigid and cramping trammels of which he had fought through in obedience to that same loyalty.  That on the one hand ; and on the other, one felt that he had passed through the ordeal of a philosophic speculation whose tendency was to obliterate or blur moral and spiritual distinctions; and he answered the subtle temptation it offered, by the demand that it should conform to the moral realities of life, or perish. ' The difference between right and wrong is real and ultimate : Christ *died* for the difference between right and wrong.'

Above all, his experience of a sin-bearing God agonising to reconcile the world in Christ was, for him, *the* ultimate reality. And ever, when he rose up from the battle of life, to meet God undertaking for him thus in love, the thrill of battle in his voice was changed to a lyrical note—the thrill of adoration. The intense and sometimes harsh note of a conscience aflame, in the search for reality, became the intense note of love aflame with redemption-gratitude. Most of us could have said—quite reverently—after the experience of his class : ' Thou hast enticed (constrained) me, and I *was* constrained : thou art stronger than I and hast prevailed.' It was a great experience, written in red and ineffaceable letters in our lives.

One thing more—besides bequeathing something of his spirit of precision—he certainly did for us : He made the New Testament the most *real* of all books to us, the record not of a dream-world apart from life, but of the highest human experience. He led us into something of the liberating greatness of that experience. ' The

New Testament,' he was fond of saying, ' is the most free-thinking book in the world.' And his own mind was advancing into the greatness of that freedom to the end. Some of his last—posthumous—pronouncements fell startlingly into some religious camps ; and the full effect of the seeds of freedom he sowed has yet to be reaped.

Because his life was lived before us always at this high-strung pitch, it was difficult for us sometimes to approach him. We never did so without much heart-searching beforehand as to whether the thing that was perplexing us was ' real.' And often, when men laid their questionings before him, they came away with a feeling of awe, as if they had been standing at the judgment seat of God.

But he was, nevertheless, intensely human. Once, in an off-moment in his home, I remember him saying with a whimsical, half-sigh that one had to brace and key oneself up when one opened one's Bible ; and one laid it down and took up *Punch, e.g.*, with a distinct and visible relaxation that was not merely mental but bodily. I am not sure now whether it was an original word of the Professor's. I think I have read something like it elsewhere. Is it in Smetham's letters ? But even so, it was a revealing word on his lips. One of the great liberating thoughts which he constantly taught is that ' Christ's Divinity was *because of*, not in

spite of, His humanity.' And yet it would seem
that in one direction at least he did not permit
himself to find a full humanity in Jesus. He
was inclined to deny altogether the presence of
a note of humour in the sayings of the Master.
His high vocation, he thought, did not permit
of it. I remember once hearing the late J. P.
Struthers of Greenock (the only man of genius,
Denney confessed to a friend after his death,
he was ever intimately acquainted with) say
that he and his great friend always differed
on this question ; he was referring in particular
to the story of the Syrophœnician woman. But
surely Struthers was right. There is a lambent—
at times almost mordant—humour, widespread
in Jesus' words. Unless laughter were an attri-
bute of Deity, one would be inclined to weep
for God in His terrible burden-bearing.

But the Professor himself had quite a distinct
sense of humour. One remembers how, at a
party, when the question was propounded,—
If one were given a choice between the gifts of
beauty and goodness, which ought one to choose ?
Dr. Denney unhesitatingly voted for beauty.
Pressed for his reason, he said, ' because if one
didn't possess beauty it was impossible of achieve-
ment : but the way was always open for a man
to *become* good ! ' And this was told me lately
by an eyewitness : he was about to board a
train one day, when a lady friend beckoned him

into the carriage beside her. 'But,' she said,
'perhaps I am doing wrong, Doctor, in enticing
you away from your comfortable first-class
carriage.' A pause and a smile. Then: 'I
never travel first-class '—another pause while
the lips twitched quizzically—' except on the
last train to Airdrie on a Saturday night!'
In public his humour usually took the form of
sarcasm, which I suppose is humour bent to
the purpose of moral or intellectual criticism.
I remember very vividly how, once, in the class,
he was warning us solemnly against the employ-
ment of sarcasm in the pulpit. ' " Sarcasm,"
says Carlyle, "is the language of the devil." '
A pause, while the lips hesitated, moving
with the burden of a momentarily suppressed
aside. Then he let it go: 'And one might
almost say it was Carlyle's mother tongue.'
The class laughed unrestrainedly; subsided;
then was swept by a second wave of merriment.
The Professor's own gravity collapsed—one of
the few times, almost the only time, he descended,
in the class, from the academic pedestal. He
laughed very self-consciously. It was a witty
stroke in itself; but in the very act of con-
demning sarcasm, he had been detected perpetrat-
ing a sarcasm himself—' hoist,' by his own hand,
' with his own petard.'

Yes, he had his very human side. But it
was no easy task for him to unbend. He had

no small change in his conversation, nothing of
the quality of the man whom Coleridge depicts
as 'given to paying his pounds in pennies.'
Yet he laboured at the task of winning his
students' confidence, of drawing them out and
getting them to talk of the things that interested
him. I remember my first invitation to his
home. In answer to his queries, I remember
telling him diffidently what an impression *Sartor
Resartus* had made on me, in the pre-university
days. 'I have been re-reading it lately,' he
said, 'reading it aloud. And it's a *great* book!'
It was easy to talk after that. But I remember
the sense of effort while we laboured to reach
common ground. *So* he always toiled—to become all things to all men, often fingering awk-
wardly a lighted cigarette while he strove, for
he was no smoker.

Yet there was an air of serenity and love in
his home, which was very restful. The sweet
woman who was queen there understood him,
and could make him show his human side as no
one else could. 'James,' she would say, 'I
think your preaching style has greatly improved
since you took to reading those French novels.'
And then would follow some delightful confessions, and criticisms of the things he had read.
I can recall him, once, in the class, discussing
the usage of the terms 'subjective' and 'objective.' He was putting us on our guard against

the elusive way they seemed to change places.
And he quoted one of those ' French novels.'
It was the description of a man who had fallen
in love, and out of it again.  He had met again
the former object of his affections.  ' He looked
at her *objectively*, as a man does at the plate off
which he has just dined well.'

What a full mind he had of all the best in
literature !  Dr. Johnson was evidently his hero
among men of letters.  We always became alert
when he began, ' as Dr. Johnson says.'  And
how penetrating, wise, and just were the literary
criticisms which fell so easily from his lips.

His appearance on the platform or in the
Assembly was always memorable.  One recalls
the passion of his earlier declarations against
Establishment.  I heard him speak at a great
Conference in Inverness after the Lords' fateful
decision of 1904.  He was blaming ' establishment ' for nearly all the worst troubles in the
history of the Church.  ' Even at the Disruption,'
he said, ' the Free Church had found difficulty
in shaking off the temper it engendered, when
she went out into the wilderness declaring she
was *the Church of Scotland*—Free.  Dr. Chalmers
himself was not immune.'  (Here a man in the
audience shouted, ' Question.')  ' A gentleman
here says, " Question."  Dr. Chalmers once
said he had been at a meeting where there
were *voluntaries and common folk* ' (other quota-

tions followed). 'That,' added Dr. Denney, vehemently rapping out his words, while the interrupter cowered in silence, 'is nothing else than the odious insolent temper of the establishment principle.'

One recalls the passion with which in an Assembly Union debate (to clear the air in which he was often summoned by the House), he called it 'an acrid poison.' Later, of course, there was a change, in method of approach, though not perhaps in principle. One of his later day utterances I have never been able quite to understand. Defending the Church of Scotland's desire to maintain the historic continuity of the National Church, he fell foul of a previous speaker, who had been distinguishing between a *de jure* and a *de facto* establishment. 'I would not,' he said, 'give an ounce of history for a ton of theory.' Where, I have often wondered since, does the nerve of history lie ? Not surely, not often at least, in legal enactments ; not in parchments laid up in the archives of Westminster, but in the life of the people of the land. Probably I had misunderstood him, for often I had heard him say—and had drunk it in as the pure milk of the word— that no Church is truly established which is not established *in the hearts and consciences of the people of the land.* The Professor would have no establishment which involved either coercion of conscience in favour of a wrong policy, or yet coercion of superstition in favour of a right.

He had grown to be the incarnation of the conscience of Scotland in his later days. One recalls how he went once with a deputation to the Glasgow magistrates to plead for the removal of licences in a certain district. He described the situation in burning sentences, tense with all the moral shame of it. ' Now who is responsible for this state of things ? ' The eyes darted a searching glance from behind the spectacles, as he made his characteristic pause. Then the long finger shot out, raking the bench of magistrates and making them squirm uncomfortably in their seats. Slowly, emphatically, decisively, this modern Nathan said : ' You gentlemen are responsible.'

Though his mind ' was like a star and dwelt apart,' he also ' the lowliest duties on himself did lay.' Every task that fell to his hands he did thoroughly. To hear him speak on the Central Fund was always a liberal education in the high principles of Christian ecclesiastical policy. It was in and for that cause he died. The situation is bad enough in Scotland to-day— through the war. One shudders to think what it might have been but for his sacrifice. ' He yet speaketh.'

He was the humblest and least assuming of men. He had a great heart. One would not speak of inmost sanctities, save in a letter, that the full impression of the beauty of his soul might be felt. But I have been told that a friend met him one day standing still in the street, his head bare, and tears on his cheeks. He said simply, it was there his beloved wife had felt the first pangs of the illness from which she died. All his public labour was the work of a great heart ; but the last years of unsparing activity were the spendings of a broken heart.

# LETTERS

I will send you something by Monday next for the *B. W.* Somehow my sermons are so undisguisedly sermonic that they don't lend themselves very readily to the purpose.

I am afraid I can't give you Corinthians for a while yet. This year of the Expositor's Bible came out so swimmingly that I thought I could give my congregation a rest from Paul: so I have not done anything for some months. However, I have finished all the difficult, at least the most difficult, and especially all the dogmatic part, and will have it done in good enough time to appear in the next series if that suits you.

Who is Rashdall, who gives the Ritschlian appreciation of Anselm and Abelard in the shape of a Univ. Serm. in *Expositor*? I think that *line* of interpretation has been taken as far as it will go now, and has yielded all it can yield ; and that it is time to rediscover the fact that the Apostles in their doctrine of atonement were dealing with something which never comes within Rashdall's (nor Ritschl's) view—namely, God's condemnation of sin as a terrifically real and serious thing. It may seem irreverent to say so, but the ' höchste einzigartige Heldenaufop-

A

ferung' theory of the atonement seems to me
simply to ignore the serious element in the
situation which the atonement is designed to
meet.  A martyrdom in plain English, no matter
how holy and loving the martyr, is an irrelevance.
I believe all evangelists would agree in that.
There is a fascinating way of presenting Abelard-
ism, but as a fisher-evangelist, a friend of mine,
once said to me, to preach it is like fishing with
a barbless hook : your bait is taken, but you don't
catch men.  The man who said that has been
greatly blessed as an evangelist, and I lay great
stress on an experience which squares so exactly,
as I think, with both the experience and the
doctrine of St. Paul.

Broughty Ferry,<br>
*November* 1, 1893.

When I read your proposal about ' Romans '
I was both flattered and taken aback; I only
hope you have not offered it to me because all
the people of reputation have declined it.  How
well or ill I could do it, it is not for me to
profess ; I think I could do it as sympathetic-
ally—I mean with as entire an appreciation of
the author—as any man, and I can promise at
all events to do it as well as I can.  I feel as
you do that there is something uncanny in mort-
gaging the future at this rate, but not being

pagans we can do it, let us hope, and still be humble. The money question I am content to leave to you. Would you mind telling me who the other contributors, or any of them, are to be ?

I hope to send Corinthians in about a month ; I am going to America about the middle or end of March, and would like to have finished the proofs, etc., by that time. I suppose that will be possible ? Of course I could send the bulk of it immediately, if you wanted it, but I have not yet written the Introduction, and cannot conveniently do so for a week or two : could you begin any other where ? I must have *some* introduction this time apart from the exposition : the questions are rather complicated which it involves.

I don't think the Chicago lectures would do for a book—so far as I can see them just now. There are to be ten : the subjects left wholly to me. What I mean to do, though the subject is systematic theology, is not anything very systematic : rather a review of the chief *loci communes theologici* with reference to current ideas, especially those of Ritschl, and also ideas not so current as they should be, especially those of the Epistles in the N. T. I will lecture on Christ's consciousness of Himself, and on the apostolic doctrine of Christ ; on Man and his condition in relation to the work of Christ, and on the work of Christ as related to the actual condition of man—there

will be two lectures, I think, on the N. T. doctrine
of Reconciliation, and on defective approaches
to it, or substitutes for it ; then I mean to have
one on the Church (the College is a Congregational
one), one (or two) on the Bible, or rather on the
word of God as a means of grace and as a spiritual
authority ; also I wish to say something on
Eschatology. Of course this is private, and open
to modification as I find the topics lend themselves to more or less elaboration as I go along.
But it will make me very busy till the winter
is over, when added to the ordinary work of a
Free Church minister. I shall be very grateful
for any suggestion that falls in at all with that
general idea of a course, or for any direction to
book or man that will help me. Fairbairn, of
course, I have read ; but with all his strenuous-
ness he does not leave on one the impression of
solidity. The constructive part of the book has
something breathless and positive about it,
which is not very convincing, and some queer
mistakes too, which both Lock and Candlish
have pointed out. I think far the most valuable
part of it is the bit immediately preceding the
constructive, the history of German philosophy
and theology in their relations to the Return to
Christ.

What bothers me a little about the Chicago
lectures is that I have no idea in the world, and
can get none, of what the men who are to hear

them already know. It is a considerable place, in size at all events : the students are resident— all theological—and last year there were 205. It was Curtiss, their Prof. of Hebrew, a man who had dealings with Delitzsch, who came here and invited me over.

I have just looked at ——'s book, and think it an odious sample of an odious kind of production—at least the first half of it. It would be a sin to advertise it on your front page by making a leader on it : but his sociology may be better than his theology.

I am going to be with Adam at Kelso on Sunday, and hope to enjoy it.

BROUGHTY FERRY,
*December* 10, 1894.

Many thanks for your note. I would by no means have a paper label on my book, though I never imagined it could affect the circulation. My objection is that it never sticks on. I leave it to you to fix up in your wisdom, always retaining the name Studies of Theology on the back in the same type as in the covers you sent : I liked it extremely : it was only my own name which seemed obtrusive.

I don't know much about legalism, and don't take to Law, except the *Serious Call.* I have only read two others of his little books : when he lapses into human nature, as in the 'characters,' I enjoy him ; otherwise his positiveness and obstinate incapacity to understand other people, and his endless argumentation about things where logic has no hold, are purely repellent to me. —— seems to reverence a man provided he cannot understand him, but I never feel inclined to be humble because a fellow-creature contrives to be unintelligible. I think there are just three ways of religion, Legalism, Evangelicalism, and Antinomianism : Evangelicals who tamper with the New Testament doctrine of atonement inevitably lapse into one or other of the bad ways. Bruce's hatred of legalism is unmistakable, but though his moral sense is the very strength of him, I don't think he appreciates sufficiently the need in his theology of this safeguard against ἀνομία.

BROUGHTY FERRY,
*July* 29, 1895.

I enclose notices of two books I had from you some time ago. Nothing has yet occurred to me coherent enough to make one of your new series out of ; I find my sermons fearfully parochial, pastoral, and for the day. If there is to be some homogeneity in the little volume, I am afraid I must make a little course of sermons on purpose, and I don't yet see the subject. When I think I do, I will let you know.

I congratulate you, in spite of the result of the elections, on the place you have made for the *B. W.* in the political as well as the religious world. You are quite an authority in places where you might hardly expect it, thanks to your candour and principle, not to mention the other things needful to command attention ; and if Liberals appreciate your last leader (as many of them do) we should show up much better in a few years. We had a very hard fight here, and great feeling, especially about the Church, but came out all right. I have been much more disappointed with the Scotch than with the English elections, and many people, depressed by the immense Toryism of England, are becoming much more interested than they once were to have Home Rule extended to Scotland.

The Established Church here make considerable use of the No-popery cry, and of the need of the establishment and the teinds to secure the Protestantism of the country ; it will be an interesting light on the situation if the Tories go in for supporting Catholic schools, whether from rates or taxes. As a rule, the R. C. people who support the Establishment, so far as I know them, are constitutionally (physically, I mean) Tories who contemn ' the mob ' and maintain everything that is, on purely selfish principles. There are plenty of them, but the strength of the Church is not in them at all, and I don't think it needs much courage to disregard them.

I had a young fellow here from Chicago last week, going to study two years in Germany. He was amazed at the universal interest in the elections—nothing else talked about in trains, hotels, streets, by men and women. There was nothing, he said, in America to compare with it at a presidential election. Of course their voting is all on one day, but even that does not seem to produce any concentrated excitement.

BROUGHTY FERRY,
*March* 11, 1897.

I wrote a letter, indeed I wrote two letters, about Greece and tore them up. I don't know why, but I could not at the time say what I wanted. I agree entirely with the line you take about the Eastern Question. To coerce Greece would be an abominable crime. The Greeks have done the only humane and heroic thing which redeems the infamy of the last three years, and to employ the resources of this country to punish them for it is an idea not to be endured for a moment. The Concert of Europe is not an end in itself. It did nothing for the Armenians —except veto every mode of interposition proposed on their behalf. It did nothing for the

Cretans. It never would have done anything. And to have it step in now, impotent for good, but irresistible for evil, is too much. What is it to us that for the sake of it we should be dragged into such shameful courses ? The latest news seems more hopeful, and if Lord Salisbury would only stiffen his back, the danger of coercion would disappear. The powers who want to coerce don't count in the Mediterranean compared with those who are against coercion in their hearts ; and the idea of Britain, France, and Italy, that have bought their own freedom at a price, combining to do the vilest work of these despotic empires, only needs to be stated to have its monstrousness appear.

What a time you are having over the Education Bill and the unprincipled Nonconformists. The Parliamentary proceedings seem at this distance simply scandalous, and though the interest in Crete tends to lessen the attention paid to them in this country, I am sure a great body of opinion is gathering, intensely hostile to the Government. Cameron's election in Glasgow by a majority of 120 instead of 1400 was as happy an omen for sound Liberalism as there has been for a good while. He was universally regarded as having betrayed that very principle of Liberalism with which he has been identified all his life for the sake of the Irish vote, and if he won that vote, it was evidently at the cost of what is a great deal more important. I was almost sorry he was returned : a man who sells himself deserves to be sold.

Have you any objection to tell me what you didn't like in my review of Stopford Brooke's O. T. Sermons ? I wrote one at your request for the *Bookman*, corrected proof, and then one by Darlow was printed. Of course I am not disputing your right not to print mine : but I would like to know whether it was the contents, or manner, or length, or what, that made it unsuitable. I must say the book did not leave a pleasant impression on my mind.

We have lovely sunny mornings now, that make one long for holidays : and clear day light till half past six—the most blessed time of the year.

[On Tuesday, May 25, 1897, the General Assembly of the United Free Church elected the Rev. Dr. James Denney Professor of Systematic and Pastoral Theology in Glasgow Free Church College. Four hundred and fifty-six members of Assembly cast their votes for Dr. Denney, and seventy-six for the Rev. John Macpherson. At the same time the Rev. Alexander Martin, M.A., Morningside Church, Edinburgh, was unanimously elected to the Chair of Apologetics in the New College, Edinburgh. Dr. Denney succeeded the late Professor Candlish, and Mr. Martin, Professor Garden Blaikie. Dr. Martin is now the honoured Principal of New College, Edinburgh.]

BROUGHTY FERRY,
*August* 21, 1897.

Your article on Hall Caine was capital. A man who is in such form ought not to get any holidays, but I could feel curious to know how Hall Caine would take it. Most authors take themselves so seriously—even Baring Gould—that in another land it might mean swords or pistols. And it is evident from the reply you printed that there are men to whom even Hall Caine is a god.

I hope you are enjoying the heavenly weather up north : I sit here a little like Giant Pope or Giant Pagan, desiring to maul the happy pilgrims who for the time have nothing to do.

21 LYNEDOCH STREET, GLASGOW,
*January* 15, 1898.

I was very willing to write the enclosed about Forsyth, not because I have not enough to do otherwise but because I liked his little book [1] very much. When the first half of it appeared in the *B. W.* I took the liberty of writing to him, though I did not know him, to say how much I appreciated it, and he made me a very friendly reply. It is a book of real experience, a rediscovery of the Gospel, worth as much as most of

---

[1] *The Holy Father and the Living Christ*, by P. T. Forsyth, D.D. (Hodder and Stoughton).

the other little books put together. I hope it will have a great circulation.

I almost wrote you at Christmas to remonstrate with you for putting in a communication about me from somebody in the class. I did not like it, and if I knew who wrote it would not be able to avoid having some prejudice against the man. You may think that unjust or a sign of incipient professorial demoralisation in me, but so it is. Up till now, I have found the work not impossible. The students have been very willing to be friendly, and appreciative of anything one has to give. Having two classes in one, which make a roll of 50, I really don't know them very well, but another year will be able to individualise more, and so, I hope, be of more service. This week I have begun the Pastl. Theol. class, and have both till the end of the session.

GLASGOW,
*November* 12, 1898.

I have written something about Dale's theology [1]—though it has limited itself, as you will see, to two points — the atonement and Christian ethics. This ran over all the space, and more, that an article usually fills; but if you like, I will write another next week about the

---

[1] The above-mentioned article on Dr. Dale's *Life*, by Professor Denney, appeared in the *British Weekly* for November 17, 1898.

Church and the Lord's Supper.[1]  The book has interested me exceedingly, but I should like to read the essay in Ecclesia before I wrote about the Supper, and that I have not yet been able to do.  Many thanks for your last letter on the subject.  I agree with all you say about the Resurrection and the Lord's body, but I do not see that that has really anything to do with the Supper.  I do not deny that there is mystery in the presence of Christ; what I objected to in Calvin, as in Luther and the Romanists, was that they made an artificial and superfluous mystery out of their own heads—a mystery at a point where no mystery should be ; and this still seems to me to be the case.  Perhaps you would not wish me, in these circumstances, to commit myself needlessly on the subject : if so, of course I shall not write anything.

21 LYNEDOCH STREET, GLASGOW,
*June* 11, 1900.

A friend of mine has written a book called a *History of Epic Poetry* (Post Virgilian).[2]  It is published by Oliver and Boyd, of all people to deal in such a commodity; and he tells me

---

[1] *Dr. Dale as a Churchman* was published on December 1 of the same year.

[2] *A History of Epic Poetry* (Post Virgilian), by John Clark, M.A. (Edinburgh : Oliver and Boyd).

that copies will be sent to the *Bookman* and the *B. W.* for review. If you have no other arrangement made, and it is not against your principles to have a man's book reviewed by his friend, I should willingly send you a short notice of it for either. But as the book deals in the Spanish and Portuguese epic, and in some other things quite off my beat, it would no doubt be possible to find a more competent hand. I believe the work is thoroughly original, and done throughout at first hand : though the writer has only an assistant mastership in the High School in Dundee, and writes badly, he is a genuine scholar, and it would be a service done to a first rate man if his book could be made visible. I hardly expect that it will have many readers.

I hope you are feeling up to the mark again. I gave your message to Grant at Nottingham, whom I got to know there for the first time, and took to extremely.

Your letter on the man who lately wrote on Wesley interested me much, as I have been reading Wesley lately. He deserved all you said about his estimate of Wesley's style, but I feel it easier to agree with you about his style than about his character. The only man of whom Wesley reminds me much intellectually is B. Franklin. They have the same relentless practicability and effectiveness in their minds, and something of the same kind of limitation.    Frank-

lin went about and saw how badly done things
were in this material world, how the street lamps
smoked inside the glass so that no light came out,
etc. etc. ; and he not only saw this, but found
out how to mend it, and could put pressure on
people to get them to mend it too.   Wesley did
the very same in the spiritual world.   His genius
was purely practical in that sphere ; he did things,
and he got them done, and that was all.   I don't
mean, of course, that that was not the greatest
of gifts, but it is only one gift, and the ever
present consciousness of infallibility which accom-
panies it strikes one as a very extraordinary
intellectual limitation, when its influence in
other directions is considered.   Nothing amused
me more, *e.g.*, than Wesley's criticisms on the
books he read.   For distinctness and emphasis
it would be impossible to surpass them, and I
daresay a man who knew all the books could
make a very interesting article on Wesley as a
literary critic ; but the infallibility is out of
place there.   It may seem impious to couple
Wesley, because of something in his mind, with
a Pharisaical old Sadducee like Franklin ; but
there is a decided intellectual affinity in them
somewhere.   With all you say about Wesley
and Law I heartily agree.   Chalmers got down
to the ground about that controversy when he
said, If God did not justify the *ungodly, what
could I do* ?

[The *Union Magazine*, edited by Dr. Orr and Dr. Denney, represented the United Free Church of Scotland, and continued the good work done for so many years by the *United Presbyterian Magazine.* Among the contributors were representative men from both Churches. The price of the Magazine was four-pence, and afterwards sixpence, and the opening number was full of attractive features. It is needless to say, wrote Claudius Clear, 'that with men so able as Dr. Orr and Dr. Denney, even the *obiter dicta* of the Magazine are always interesting.]

21 LYNEDOCH STREET, GLASGOW,
*January* 4, 1901.

It was very obliging of you to give us such a friendly and helpful notice as you have in this week's *B. W.*,[1] and I am most grateful for it. I would have sent you a proof of your article about Aberdeen College, but I knew you were from home and looked over it myself. We have arranged for some others on what are meant to be the same lines, but as everything depends on how they are written, I am not without misgivings. It needs a skilful and practised hand to do the thing in a style which has any attraction, and that is rare. I think all the reviews in this number were written by Orr and myself, so that if there is any terrible

[1] The *Union Magazine* was reviewed by Claudius Clear in his letter of Jan. 3, 1901.

responsibility to bear in connection with them its distribution is comparatively simple. But do you think in such a case we should really sign them ? It would be too monotonous.

What I feel most difficulty about is the extent to which we should write in it ourselves. We want to have all subjects of interest to the Church discussed in it by competent people, but I dread its degenerating into aimlessness unless some one takes charge of it to a greater extent, and gives it a purpose, if not a policy. If you have any idea that would help us here I should consider it thankfully.

I was interested to see you putting in a word for Mansel in the *British Monthly.* I have always felt like you about him, that so strong-headed a man had a case, and was not to be easily dismissed from the field as he has been by philosophers and theologians alike. He saw and felt (what is the truth) that agnosticism is an element in true religion, and a pervading element in it ; where he erred was perhaps in exaggerating this truth so as to give the impression that agnosticism was really the principle of religion. But between gnostic philosophers, like those who succeeded him in Oxford, and agnostics who think that their philosophy rivals or excludes religion, he had hold of a piece of the truth, and will no doubt get his due when all is done.

We have had our usual holiday here, such as

B

can be had in a rainfall exceeding anything known for 120 years : so at least they told us at Crieff, where we were for a week.

21 Lynedoch Street, Glasgow,
*January* 11, 1901.

I am much in your debt for all your suggestions about the Magazine and will try to act on them and to get the other editor to do so also. I entirely agree with you about the Topic, and I feel generally that to have too many ' series ' of things going on, and turning up in every number, must be fatal. But I had no idea of doing a whole series myself! The paper on 'Anger' I had in last number was the first of a set to be done by different men, and I only did the first because there was no other at hand. Some good men have promised contributions, and I hope we may be able to make it readable, more or less.

I am sending with this the first half of a discussion of sin in Romans : I found that the whole thing would be absurdly long for one article ; and this, which deals with the conceptions of sin and law, but leaves the experience of the sinner under law and the questions raised in connection with Chs. 5 and 7 to be dealt with in another paper, has a certain unity in itself.

THE UNION MAGAZINE,
*January* 29, 1901.

If the old men in the Church die at the rate at which they have done lately, we shall not want for 'historic interest.' I think in the notices of such this month there is one which is extraordinarily well done, to be a suggestion of a man whose life had no events of public interest. It is signed A. P., and is by Mr. Philip of Invergowrie—on his predecessor, Mr. Hunter. I knew the old gentleman, whose son was an elder in my church, and can certify its truth.

21 LYNEDOCH STREET, GLASGOW,
*February* 22, 1901.

Your two letters have such a lot of things in them that I hardly know where to begin to answer.

I have been thinking about Schmiedel, and am not quite sure whether he ought to be treated as a deadly enemy of the Christian faith (he certainly throws it all away), or as an entirely irresponsible person. The one sentence you quote from him in the *British Monthly*, about the Johannine question entering on a new phase (the Simon Magus one), is only a specimen of hundreds as good; once you discount all that follows upon the rejection of the supernatural on principle, most of what remains in Schmiedel, in spite of an occasional acuteness, is infinitely more absurd than ingenious. If it were worth the trouble it would be very interesting to compare his view of the Gospels with Abbott's : except in their common rejection of the supernatural, I question if they have much in common. Anyhow, there is nothing I should like better to hear than Schmiedel's opinion of Abbott's single, double, and triple tradition, and so forth. The publication of two such articles side by side is a sign of extraordinary courage or of sheer despair. I don't believe that the Christian religion—let alone the Church—can live unless we can be sure of (1) a real being of God in Christ ; (2) the atoning death ; (3) the exaltation of Christ. All these are embodied in the apostolic testimony to Christ, and indeed are omnipresent in it ; but I am not sure that they are all represented in their full dimensions in the Gospels—*i.e.* I am not sure that the Gospels represent the whole of the apostolic testimony, and therefore I could not think of basing Christianity on them alone, if it is to have a documentary basis at all. It needs the whole of the New Testament to show what Christ is, and a man only deceives himself when he goes *behind Christianity,* and exhibits as the historical Jesus a figure which could never have created Christianity at all. The ineffectiveness of Schmiedel's Christ to do what the historical Christ undeniably did proves that his is not the historical Christ at all.  For the public at large, it is only in this general way the subject could be considered :  the arguments for and against the Johannine authorship of the Fourth Gospel must be left to experts.  The only thing in connection with the three essentials of Christianity mentioned above in which there is any ambiguity is the first :  the certainty of a real being or presence of God in Christ does not, so far as apostolic testimony allows us to judge, imply anything as to the mode of the incarnation.  The Gospels of the infancy are in harmony with it, but it might be held (and the sinlessness of Jesus too) in independence of them.

21 LYNEDOCH STREET, GLASGOW,
*March* 1, 1901.

Struthers has practically prohibited me from saying anything about him, and has indicated his reluctance (which I hope he will overcome) to have the *Watch* [1] issued in London.  He spoke in the kindest possible way about your letter to him, but regards being written about with the sensations of a whelk being wormed out of its shell on a pin point.  But there can be no harm in telling what everybody knows—that he is a minister of the Reformed Presbyterian Church of Scotland, *not* an

[1] The *Morning Watch*, edited by the Rev. J. P. Struthers, of Greenock.

Original Seceder; that he preaches for anybody who asks him, and gets only too much of it to do; that he *is* a good preacher, the most solemn and the most tender you could imagine, as any one could infer from the *Watch*; and that his age may be guessed (it is only so that I have any idea of it) from the time when he was ordained—which according to the *Clerical Almanac* was 1878. His congregation is not large, but his church is full.

I was very much interested by all you told me about Abbott. His analysis of the Gospels is as utterly unscientific as anything could be, and I don't think it is difficult to see that Schmiedel thinks so. When I said it showed either great courage or sheer despair to print both, what I meant was that the utter inconsistency of the two made the presentation of both, side by side, either a sort of bravado, or a confession that the editors ' gave up ' the synoptic problem. However, Schmiedel is the only one of the two who needs to be taken seriously, and I have an idea of writing something about him in the next number of the *Union Magazine*. It is just Strauss over again, but without a spark of the wit or genius—a pedantic Strauss, who leaves on the mind the impression of a man who has learned to spell, but not to read—or who believes that the life of Christ is in the letters of the dictionary, and that it is merely a matter of putting them properly together to produce the force which has created Christianity. What the responsibility of Black or Cheyne can be for it I don't know ; but I should like to know what Schmiedel conceives his own relation to Christianity to be : and if he thinks it a ' clear case that there is nothing in it,' why he should have been asked to do this piece of work by men who must be assumed to believe in the Christian religion.

In the circumstances you must not expect me to write about him in the *B. W.* It is of course an infinitely better place to write in than our poor little Church paper, but I am reduced to the necessity of doing it for the latter and could only repeat myself—as I have had to do with Moffatt.

21 Lynedoch Street, Glasgow,
*January* 9, 1902.

I ought to have acknowledged at once the *Church's One Foundation* : it is very good of you to send me the book. I am at the subject all the time, and can therefore, I hope, appreciate the seriousness of it; and, as you know, I agree with you in everything in it which is of real importance. What troubles me is not how to blow the trumpet, or sound an alarm, but how to teach in detail, and persuade people who are alarmed not to close their minds in impatience, but to face the kind of questions criticism raises, and to *meet* them with the composure of intelligence, as well as the assurance of faith.   One tries to do it in teaching, and with time and pains it can be done, but who will give time and pains ?   I hope we are not in for a time of panic, or of apathy either, but may be brought through the strait into a larger room.

What you said in a ' letter ' lately in the *B. W.* about the ' interestedness ' of good editors was what struck me most in turning over your other book : it is so desperately easy to look at things, and even people, without seeing them, or to get valuable hints and be unconscious of them.   I am glad to see you are in the third edition already. That, by the way, reminds me that some weeks ago I saw in the *Glasgow Herald* an advertisement of my *Studies* in the 5th edition, whereas I lifted one in a shop the other day marked 6th edition, completing 11th thousand, and dated 1899— which I suppose is correct.  Your pious hope that I will put the lectures on the Death of Christ into *The Expositor* can hardly be fulfilled : but I would like to revise them in the summer, and have them published in autumn.  There is nothing in them but an exhibition of the New Testament teaching; but the centrality and gravity and inevitableness and glory of it impressed me more than ever, and I think it is worth insisting on.  The epistles deduce everything Christian from it, theological and ethical; and there is no choice but to take it or leave it.

I have been trying to get interesting historical matter for the *Union Magazine*, but you see with what success. Next month we are to have an article on Dr. Aird of Criech by a man who knew him well and got all his papers, but there is not much in it. I have one promised also on Mr. Cumming of Melness, by a lady, which one may hope will have a sense of what is interesting in character. But no one, apparently, can write who has not made a study of it; and the circle to which we can appeal for contributors does not contain many who have. Most sermons must be extempore compositions.

At Christmas we spent a week at St. Andrews, and I did what I venture to say you have never done in your life—spent the whole seven days without once dipping a pen in ink. Neither did I use a Swan fountain, but wrote no word to enemy or friend.

Mrs. Denney is happy again in her restored *Watches*, and joins me in wishing you a happy new year.

21 LYNEDOCH STREET, GLASGOW,
*July* 29, 1902.

I am posting along with this the MS. of which we have spoken before.[1] It is in length, so far as I can judge, almost exactly equal to George Smith's Yale Lectures;[2] and I should like it printed in something like that fashion, or like one of Dale's books. Instead of an index, to which it does not readily lend itself, I have put in a sort of outline of each chapter in the contents, which will enable any one to see the line of the thing and to find what he wants if it is there. For a title, I should like it called either 'The Death of Christ: its Place and Interpretation in the New Testament'; or, 'The Death of Christ in the New Testament: its Place and Interpretation.'

I hope you can come to see us when you are in Scotland. We go to Pitlochry on Friday, and will be there till the end of August. Dr. Orr was proposing the other day to try the *Union Magazine* at 6d.; if we do anything different with it, I fancy it must rather be 3d. I should like to hear your mind about it—not the price only, but other things. I have a growing conviction that editing must be made one's business if it

[1] *The Death of Christ,* by Professor James Denney, D.D. (Hodder and Stoughton, 1902).
[2] Dr. George Adam Smith.

is to come to anything, and that no one can do it in the bygoing. Not that I ever indulged any such delusion, but even a little experience has made me proof against it if I had.

How the Nonconformists seem to want a man of weight just now like Dale! Fairbairn can never be an Englishman, with all his ability, and there could not be a more fatal drawback to any one wishing to deal with an English question. The political weakness seems to me to be that while the High Church party has principles as well as the Nonconformists, so that in this respect they are equally matched, the Liberal party, through which the Nonconformists have to act, has at present no principles at all—I mean no religious ones—and is therefore an ineffective instrument. It does not naturally care for spiritual religion as the Tory party naturally cares for the Established Church, so that in the field of action the Nonconformists have all the advantages against them. I am afraid, unless it comes as you suggest to fines and imprisonments all over, they will just be trampled on.

I forgot to say that I had made up my mind not to reprint the articles on Romans with this. Partly because the subject has a completeness in itself, partly because there is a slight amount of repetition at one point, and partly because I could not think what to call it. Practically I believe it will do more good as it is.

21 Lynedoch Street, Glasgow,
*October* 16, 1902.

I want to ask a considerable favour from you. Could you spare the most of a page of the Scotch edition of the *British Weekly* to print the enclosed—the address which I gave at the opening of the College yesterday? I wrote it for the present distress, and should like it to be read by more people in the Church than heard it, and you can give the only effective help, if you think it worth while. If not, may I ask you, in spite of all your rules, to let me have it back?

We are watching here with the closest interest your action on the Education Bill. If any man is entitled to the credit of the national movement, it is you, and one could only wish for Liberalism a leader with any principle or backbone to take the guidance of it, or responsibility for acting on it. The other side are strong only because we are weak; and the only sign that they are a little frightened is Chamberlain's visit to Birmingham, and Balfour's loss of temper. It is not like the popular ideal of him to speak of ' deliberate mendacity.' A few more bye-elections like Sevenoaks and North Leeds would be very opportune.

We have begun this session with 20 regular students in the first year—two of them Ferguson scholars. It is a mercy to have quality when quantity fails.

21 LYNEDOCH STREET, GLASGOW,<br>
February 19, 1903.

Your faith amazes me. These lectures are like a cloud in front of me, but I cannot *sit down* to think of them till the session is over, and what will come out of it when I do I have no idea. They might be what I should wish to publish or wish to hide, but if they are likely to do anybody any good, I will certainly think of your assistance in circulating them. Have you any idea of what ' the modern mind ' is ? Is it the same as the *Zeitgeist* ? or is it something with much more of truth and eternity in it than that ? It strikes me that the question about the relation of the modern mind to the atonement is only one phase of the larger question of the relation of reason to revelation, or of human nature to God—a question on which it is easier to say what seem profound philosophical things than to say things which really have power either to convince or persuade. But it is no use talking vaguely before the time.

I hope you had a good holiday and that your letter in this week's *B. W.* is not *urgently* autobiographical. Here we have had frightful

weather, but begin to scent the spring, and feel
that we will not go under before it comes.

Mr. Carroll, of St. John's Church here, an
old friend of mine, and a life-long student
of Dante, has written a book on the 'Inferno'[1]
which he would like to have published, and
asks me to write to you about it. Carroll
is one of the most gifted men I know, has been
much in Italy, knows Dante not through translations merely, nor commentators, but with an
intimacy which if it is not balanced by a strong
sense of proportion might qualify him to write a
book which only enthusiasts would read; but
I believe he has the faculty to keep proportion,
and I should expect his book to be really valuable.
May he send it to you, and have your mind about
publishing it ?   I don't know whether it is a line
which Hodder and Stoughton would wish to
cultivate—I fancy it is a precarious public to
count upon ;  but if they should, I am sure Carroll
would be a creditable supporter.   He has written
a few short papers for us in the *Union Magazine*,
but they are slight and give no idea of his power.

[1] Dr. Carroll's work on the 'Inferno' was published by Messrs.
Hodder and Stoughton, under the title *Exiles of Eternity*.  The firm
also published his work on the 'Purgatorio,' *Prisoners of Hope*,
and on the 'Paradiso,' *In Patria*.

15 Lilybank Gardens, Glasgow,
*June* 12, 1903.

I have been immersed in the chaos of ' flitting,' or would have answered you sooner.
The three lectures I have to give at Aberdeen
are now finished, and I will send you them
when I have read them there. They are rather
long, severally, for *Expositor* articles, and too
short, collectively, to make even a very little
book on religion ; but if you think they would
be interesting or useful I should have no objection to their being printed. There is nothing in
them about ' the powers of evil '—not that I do
not think there is anything to say, but I do not
think it is an aspect of the facts which the modern
mind finds very accessible. I read Nordau and
Merejowski : in the latter I was much interested,
though I cannot say much has remained in my
mind except the abstract contrast between
Tolstoy and Dostoevsky, which, like all such
abstract contrasts, is as false at least as it is true.
Merejowski is evidently, like Plato, a most poetic
philosopher, and one who could compete with
the dramatists on their own ground, but, as far
as he has a way of thinking of his own, I do not
see in the least how to bring Christianity into
contact with it. The one thing in him with
which I profoundly agreed, and which I had long
felt quite apart from him, is that the things or

aspects of things which we call natural and spiritual do not exist at all except in and through each other. That truth, I am confident, is at the bottom of the simplest statement of the atonement—Christ *died* for our *sins*. If death was *only* physical, and if sin and the divine reaction against it were *only* moral, these words would have no meaning. There must be a ' mystical union ' of the natural and the spiritual in sin if this is the condition of redemption from it.

15 LILYBANK GARDENS, GLASGOW,
*July* 1, 1903.

With this you will get the three lectures I gave in Aberdeen. There are, I should say, 24,000 (or thereby) words in them. This might be enough to make a little book on religion, if you thought it worth while to use them so after publication in *The Expositor*: I should rather like that those who bought the *Death of Christ* should be able to have this also in a convenient way, as it is partly of the nature of a supplement—at one or two points an explanation or defence—of what I have said there.

The School was quite a success,—a large gathering and very hearty. Everybody, of course, wanted opportunity for discussion, and the committee, when they try again, will have this in mind ; but with only a few hours altogether, discussion is apt to be too engrossing, and the one purpose such a gathering can serve—to bring men who have been out of the way up to time—might easily be defeated.   I have a class in which there is always opportunity for discussion, and usually discussion as well ; but what you can do with men whom you meet several times a week may not be so profitable in a chance audience.

Smith [1] has had a very bad time, but is getting better.   He must walk softly, which he is not used to, for a long time to come.

15 LILYBANK GARDENS, GLASGOW,
*November* 18, 1903.

Miss Wallace, whom you know about, has had a story printed in the *Union Magazine* this year, which she wants to publish as a book.   She asked me to write to you about it, and I could not refuse, though I told her it could make no difference either to you or the story.   She calls it *The Harvest of a Dream*, and seems to love it : if she sends it to you, you will know to what I refer.

I hope you are keeping well this winter.   As a rule I have a Johnsonian indifference to atmospheric conditions, but the endless rains of this autumn came as near to making me melancholy as any weather I have ever known.   Smith,

[1] Dr. George Adam Smith.

C

you will know, has sailed for India : his work is divided between Eaton and Welch. He had been dreadfully ill, and though he was up to his old weight before he left he seemed strangely pithless—for *him*. I sincerely hope the year off may do him all the good he needs : we miss him dreadfully at the hall.

Last month MacEwen in Edinburgh and I in Glasgow gave notice of overtures to the Assembly about the curriculum. What the Assembly will do if the overtures go up I have no idea : to appoint a Committee will likely be everything, to begin with. What we both have in view— don't laugh—is a substantial addition to the length of the session. I have found out already that there will be opposition to it in two at least of the Colleges, if not three ; but nevertheless I have hope that something may be achieved. The universities are feeling the need of it too, and may move at the same time. The one discouraging thing is that every one who hears of the session being lengthened immediately assumes that the four years' curriculum must be reduced to three. It may be difficult to stick to four when the Established Church has three, and the U.P.'s were accustomed to it, but the last year, even though we make little use of it, does make most men less unfit to be ministers.

15 LILYBANK GARDENS, GLASGOW,
*November* 28, 1903.

It was very good of you to write me so long
a letter, and I am correspondingly grateful.
But you must not imagine that you could
harrow my soul by anything you say about
theological education. I question whether you
are as revolutionary about this as I am, and
I was very much interested to find that all the
points you touched on had in one way or another
been forced on my attention before. Last year,
at a meeting of the association of former students
connected with our College, I opened a discussion
on the training of ministers, and a few weeks ago
I gave an address on the same subject to the
students in the hall at Aberdeen—all the professors except Johnstone being present. Iverach compared it good-humouredly to Chamberlain's fiscal speeches—the work of a person who
is quite clear, quite sure that he is right, very
plausible, but entirely, hopelessly, and, if he
cannot be suppressed, fatally wrong. I went
generally on the line that what we want in
ministers is educated men and Christians, but
argued that the ways of being educated are now
so varied, compared with what they once were,
that our narrow compulsory system ought to be
revised and largely antiquated. A minister
ought to be a specialist in something, no doubt,

but the something is not, or need not be, either textual or historical criticism, on which we waste a disproportionate amount of our time. We could teach a great deal more that would fit men to be ministers if we did not indulge the pretence of teaching through Greek and Hebrew instead of teaching in the mother tongue. You seem to reserve your animosity for Hebrew : I am quite prepared, if a man comes up with an M.A. degree which does not include the subject, to extend it to Greek. Of course I don't think either Greek or Hebrew worthless, nor do I think the Church should be without them, or fear that it will be : but I do think it no better than a superstition to believe that every man who is to preach the Gospel and do pastoral work must affect to be a student of Greek. In our present first year there are men who have honours in chemistry, zoology, mathematics and natural philosophy, and we generally have some now who have economics or history in their degree ; all these are just as good instruments of culture as Greek or Hebrew ; and as for finding the word of God in Holy Scripture, and presenting it for the edifying of the Church, the men who cannot do that with the English Bible—which is all that the Church itself has to depend upon—cannot do it at all. I entirely agree with you about English too, and spoke of it at Aberdeen. I have fortnightly papers written by my classes, and the correction of them is as much teaching English grammar and composition as anything else. It is not always that they have no ideas, but there is not one man in a score who can say what he means. Partly from impotence and partly from ambition, they are totally unable to put their minds plainly on paper. But though all this is sad truth, I do not hope for much more than an extension of the session, and it may not be quite easy to get even that.

About the *Atonement*, I have no desire nor intention to say more at present,[1] but I will be interested to hear what Peake says. To reduce St. Paul to moral commonplace is very far from my intention, but I must frankly say that between soaring above the intelligible and sinking beneath it there does not seem to me to be much to choose : and when a man maintains that there is something which may be described as a ' mystical union,' which transcends a moral union, all I can say is that my mind does not follow him. I cannot conceive anything which transcends a moral union. There is a mystical union, if you like, between a stone and God, but the union of man and God transcends the mystical and rises out of it, into the region of the intelligible and moral. It does not seem to me to be clipping or sweating the spiritual coinage to say this : on

---

[1] Dr. Denney's work, *The Atonement and the Modern Mind* (Hodder and Stoughton), was published in 1903.

the contrary, much of what appears (in St. Paul)
to favour the idea of a mystical as going beyond
a moral union is the language of passion, which
has a poetic and emotional truth—a kind of truth
which is necessary to religion—but which *loses*
its truth the moment it is turned into prose.  It
is just like the language of passion in which the
sacramental bread and wine are called the body
and blood of Christ.  No other language would
satisfy Christian feeling.  Yet they are *not* the
body and blood of Christ, and a great deal that
is written about the mystical union seems to me
as unreal as transubstantiation.  Probably there
will always be differences here due to differences
of temperament, some men having more need
than others for particular modes of expression.

I hope nothing may hinder you from writing
the series of papers you propose on the Atonement and Modern Literature.  Few people read
theology and everybody reads novels, and you
have the art of speaking both to the few and the
many.  I used to be annoyed in Oliver Wendell
Holmes with his insistence on physiology in
morals, and should hardly think it so important
as you seem to do.  But are you not wrong in
saying that he ' took up Darwin's conclusions as
showing that the area of responsibility is far more
contracted than the theologians imagined,' etc. ?
Holmes never had a word more to say than he
said in the *Autocrat*, and the *Autocrat* is a year

older than the *Origin of Species*. Personally, I
always feel that the ultimate effect of Darwinism
must be to enlarge indefinitely the area of responsibility, and in some ways the general conscience is coming to recognise this too. When
we look *back* in the Darwinian light, our responsibility seems less ; but when we look *forward*, if
we acknowledge responsibility at all, as every one
does, whatever his philosophy, then our responsibility is enormously increased. Everything that
intensifies this feeling will work in the long run
to make the atonement credible, and I feel pretty
sure that the common conscience, while it may
be fully as ready as it once was to impute its
burdens to its ancestry, is more sensitive than it
was about transmitting them to posterity. When
you begin your articles you can count on an
interested public.

15 LILYBANK GARDENS, GLASGOW,
*January* 5, 1904.

I am posting with this the article on Harnack
and Loisy. It is an interesting duel, and I wish
Harnack could find leisure to say something
more. He seems to me the better Christian of
the two, but they are both anxious to run a
very big concern on a quite inadequate capital.

I see what you mean about Mark Rutherford,
and agree ; but do you think it is true to say—

' this is the good in life which is in a manner within the reach of all '? Sometimes one is tempted to think that there is nothing which is so little within people's reach as this deliverance through love. What an immense number of women there are in this country who never get the chance of it, or any chance they can take, and who when they get to about eight and twenty begin to be a little bitter and irritable and generally sceptical about all things. What a number of people, too, don't really get it even when they marry—they get the music of the fiddle, as Ibsen says, where there are always strings breaking and needing to be mended, but not the thrilling passionate music of the bell, which once cracked (he seems to think it is mostly cracked) can never be mended. It was partly with this in my mind that I did not emphasise love in the Deliverance. Resignation and doing good are open doors to everybody in a sense in which love is not. About Mark Rutherford's own history I know nothing, and I was not attracted by his interest in the incompatibilities, especially in his later books. Clara Hopgood I thought detestable.

The year is too new yet to have yielded any news. We are living in a reign of interdicts and responses which seem intended only to illustrate the malignity and unscrupulousness of the ' Free ' Church, and the imbecility of the law. When we will see the end of it I cannot imagine. Churches may be annexed to any extent to which the minority please before Parliament can do anything, and if they like to spend the capital of the funds in their hands the minority may keep them going for a while. I did not think that such unprincipled and unscrupulous scoundrelism as is being deliberately planned and practised every day was within the limits of possibility in men who had Bibles and affected an unusual reverence for them. It really looks as if they thought the highness of their creed could cover any depth of lowness in their conduct.

15 Lilybank Gardens, Glasgow,
*February* 10, 1904.

. . . I am glad you feel the better of your holiday, for your work in the *B. W.* is cut out for you. There has not been such an approach to political chaos in my memory, and the levity of the responsible people in face of Russian wars and education iniquities and Chinese slavery and Protectionist bribing of the people *seriatim* at the cost of swindling them *en masse* is enough to make one despair. I heard Campbell-Bannerman when he was here lately. He was in remarkably good spirits, spoke wisely, and wittily, and had a great reception : but there was not enough of momentum in it. In-

deed there was no momentum at all. He spoke
like a man who was happy in having an excellent
case, not like a man with a cause—it is the want
of such a man that is the ruin of Liberalism just
now. Positively I have had more hope of the
Duke of Devonshire than of any other man on
the scene. Can you offer me a job if the House
of Lords gives my salary to the true Free Church ?


15 Lilybank Gardens, Glasgow,
*February* 19, 1904.

I cannot find words to express my sense of
the extraordinary kindness of your letter of
yesterday. It would never have occurred to
me to put labour or responsibility on anybody
else, least of all on any one so occupied as you
are, in connection with the collapse of the
*Union Mag.* At present I can only thank you,
as I do most heartily, for your interest in our
poor concerns : when I have seen Dr. Orr, and
talked it over with him, I will write again with
more particulars of the situation. But I ought
to thank your publishers too, even in this note ;
it is exceedingly generous of them to make the
offer which they do. My first feeling, or next
after the first, was, as I told you, one of relief.
I dislike as much as Swift or anybody to hear
men talking of how much they have to do ; but
I have to lecture twelve hours a week, spend as

much time on students' papers—not perhaps a wise investment for me, but the only way in which I can get work out of a lot of them—preach every Sunday, and either do or refuse to do a crowd of other things, besides the reading and writing which are one's proper business ; and I frankly say that the unfortunate and inevitable *Magazine* sometimes came near being the last straw. You know that the first thing in that kind of work is speed, and I am not speedy in anything, and apparently cannot acquire it. But I share strongly your opinion that it is a pity to see the Christian religion beaten out of the region in which people generally lead their intellectual life ; and adding to this the aversion of the natural man to being beaten, my inclination would be, if things should make it practicable, to try again. What Dr. Orr may say I do not know, but I should think he would be favourable. His connection with the *Magazine* was older, and his affection for it more sentimental than mine. If it is to be suspended for a little while anyhow, perhaps I might see you before anything further has to be decided.

I have to be in Oxford some time in May in connection with Welsh University Examinations ; and could easily take a run to London when there.

15 LILYBANK GARDENS, GLASGOW,
*March* 16, 1904.

With this I send a paper apropos of Gardner and Jülicher, or rather of Gardner alone : Jülicher is a book one could only treat in detail. It is heavy, I fear, but this reconstruction of the New Testament has got to a point at which what we want most is a statement of first principles—such as might be evolved if the Harnack and Loisy duel were fought out to the end. The tacit presupposition of much criticism is that Jesus was just another man; and the astonishing thing is that in the circumstances, with this one essential point fixed in advance, people should imagine that there is still anything particular in the New Testament to talk about. What we want, along with a consideration of first principles, is a statement of the mind of Christ about Himself : I feel as sure as I can be of anything that to this the Christian religion will be driven back, and I am equally sure that there it is impregnable, both ' historically ' and ' spiritually.'

We have not yet finished up the affairs of the *Union Magazine* so as to be able to show you exactly how it stood, but Dr. Orr, who is looking after it, hopes to be able to do so soon. If I did not tell you before, I ought to do so now, that he appreciates as highly as I do your extraordinary kindness in connection with it.

*Cerach*

I thought Carnegie Simpson did Dods very
well in the *British Monthly*. If he goes to
Canada I shall be sorry, as he is a near neighbour
here and a friend.

15 LILYBANK GARDENS, GLASGOW,
*May* 28, 1904.

I have made up my mind with much regret
to decline your generous offer about restarting
the *Union Magazine*. The more I thought of
it, the more I appreciated your kindness, but
the more also I became convinced that the
work was not for me. You will think I will
not do anything better with the time I spent on
it, or any the more at all because I have so much
the less to do, but this is the conclusion to which
I have come. Dr. Orr, you may know, is very
anxious to continue, and unless you feel precluded
by the possibilities involved in the circular which
I enclose, I hope you can make the proposal to
him alone which you made to us jointly. About
this circular I have not been able to find out
much. I asked Erskine, the printer, about it,
and he said he was not at liberty to mention the
names which were behind it, but he alluded in-
advertently to MacEwen and Ross Taylor, though
Ross Taylor, he said, wished to remain in the
background. From these names I should be
disposed to infer that the new move is being

engineered by people who do not agree with the line Orr and I took upon public questions : but I do not know for certain.  In the course of next week, the meeting to which the circular refers will probably be held, and it will be apparent then whether anything can be done to make a fresh start on a three-penny basis.  A paper like the *Young Man,* with 46 pp. and 4 pp. of inset advertisements, is Erskine's notion of what is wanted ; as he has had the circulation of it for twelve years he perhaps knows what people are willing to pay.

The Natural Science Chair had a narrow squeak for life—at least the regular professorship had. Iverach spoke strongly for a full session of teaching on the relations of science and religion instead of the forty lectures we get at present, as if the one fundamental fault of our system was not that students get far too many lectures already, and that in any rearrangements we make the number must be diminished, not increased. I have written an article on the training of a minister for the next *London Quarterly* ; I should expect you to agree with it as far as it goes.

15 LILYBANK GARDENS, GLASGOW,
*July* 10, 1904.

. . . It was very good of you to write as you did again about the *Union Magazine,* and I

am more grateful than I can say; but the more
I think of it the clearer it seems that it is not
a work to which I have any call. I would
gladly be a contributor on occasion, if it could
be undertaken by anybody else, but the regular
responsibility of it does not suit either my
faculties or my other engagements. It is with the
more regret I say this, that Dr. Orr's interest in
it is quite keen, and that there will no doubt
come occasions in our Church life when such a
mode of address would be particularly useful;
but I hope you can believe that I have done my
best not to be selfish in deciding. I wish you
could find some younger and more fertile mind
and make the same generous offer to him.

Last week I was in Aberystwyth and heard
Silvester Horne and Jones of Bournemouth.
They had an enthusiastic audience and made good
speeches. The Church evidently counts for far
more in Aberystwyth than in Glasgow. Who
could get a crowd here on a summer night to hear
about Free Church principles or any other
principles?

15 Lilybank Gardens, Glasgow,<br>July 12, 1904.

You must marvel at my infirmity of purpose,
and I need not try to explain it. I really did
not think, nor do I think yet, that this *Magazine*

work is a thing I am meant for; but I feel what a good thing it might be, and what decided me at the last moment to try again was rather the feeling that I was keeping the light from being quenched than that I could ever fan it into a flame. Possibly if it is kept from going out for a year or two some man may appear with the gift and the will to tend it : if so, I will gladly resign my place to him.

When I saw you, I forgot to speak about advertisements, which used to be a good part of the income : but I presume Hodder and Stoughton will look after these, as well as all about paper, printing, producing of pictures, etc. ; and that our business—I mean Dr. Orr's and mine—will be solely the providing of the literary matter, and the photos, or whatever else the pictures are to be taken from. The one dread I have about it, apart from the labour, is that it is too small for the money, that people will not give 6d. for it, and that the publishers will lose by it ; and, though you have said everything that kindness could say to mitigate that apprehension, it comes back on one's mind, and if it were to be realised would certainly make one feel unhappy. However, I am truly anxious to save the life of the thing, if I can, and you will understand this, I hope, in spite of vacillations.

15 LILYBANK GARDENS, GLASGOW,
*August* 4, 1904.

With this I am sending some observations on
Hastie's book.[1] It is not a very good subject,
but it may give you an idler day in August,
and I am sure you want one. So do I. It is
curious how Hastie touches on a number of the
subjects which the House of Lords has made
so interesting, and in what I have said I have
referred principally to these. Hastie's death is
a great loss to the Established Church.

The sensation of the judgment is spreading as
the significance of it in detail comes home to
people's minds. Some, like Rainy, think its
seriousness cannot be exaggerated ; others, with
Sheriff Guthrie, do not see the need of putting so
grave a face upon it. *Some* settlement must be
made—so they say : and when matters come to
a point they may not be so bad after all. I
entirely agree with the strain in which you have
written about it, and I am quite sure that whatever happens there will be no thought of giving
up ' spiritual independence.' Whatever may be
thought of it in the House of Lords, it is the one
thing which everybody in the Church understands,

[1] *The Theology of the Reformed Church in its Fundamental Principles,*
by Rev. Dr. Hastie, Professor of Divinity in Glasgow University.
The work was published after Dr. Hastie's death, with an introduction
by Professor Flint. Dr. Denney's article on it, entitled ' A State
Church Theologian,' appeared in the *British Weekly* of August 25,
1904.

D

and I have not come across anybody who does not see that when it is refused there is no longer any such thing as a Church. What I dread most is what I feel most—the temptation to indulge one's temper, and to say what one feels about representatives and supporters of the other side. But I hope the magnitude of the crisis will help everybody to behave worthily. What you say about the parties agreeing to promote an Act of Parliament will find very general support. We, of course, have nothing to offer, and nothing to negotiate upon—like a Free Trade government dealing with tariff-walled nations ; but it will be possible to get into relations with the appellants somehow, and to see what they want to do or to get. The people for whom I feel most are the ministers and members in the Highlands who adhered to the Union, and will have to lose their churches and manses in consequence. The loss of a great part of our bursary funds, too, might be very embarrassing at the Hall, for many students cannot do without them. Whether Free Church Professors will have any salaries left them, and if so what, remains to be seen : meanwhile we have nothing. I believe what would be *felt* more than anything as a kind of insult within the injury would be the appropriation of the Assembly Hall and the New College. It must be tempting for the appellants to seal their triumph visibly in some such way : but perhaps Glasgow College would suit them better. We are in some way entirely in their hands. As for an Act of Parliament, I believe Balfour would do anything reasonably within his power to conciliate good will in Scotland : he needs all he can get. And Balfour of Burleigh would help him, knowing that any liberty legally secured to our Church would also be legally secured for his : at least he would feel that we could not decently oppose its extension even to the Establishment. But there may be a good while of suspense, and the need of raising another £30,000 a year to carry on the work which has hitherto depended on endowments.

THE HOTEL, ABINGTON,<br>LANARKSHIRE, September 9, 1904.

You may be away before this gets to London, but I take the risk. You know I can only welcome any suggestions about the *Magazine*, and I am much indebted for those in your last letter. The only thing in your letter which doesn't quite commend itself is the suggestion about Mark Rutherford. All his books make a strong impression, but to me it is an intensely disagreeable one, and I would rather forget than digest it. No doubt that is cowardly and immoral, but it is instinctive—which you may say only makes it worse. If any one sent a good article I should willingly accept it, but I do not feel moved to look for one, or to attempt one myself.

15 LILYBANK GARDENS, GLASGOW,
*October* 8, 1904.

Your letter was as much of an astonishment to me as R. R. Simpson and Lawson's was to you, and with all that you say about the latter I cordially agree. I anticipated, as you know, that people might find fault with us for using the name of the Church, but I thought only of irresponsible persons who might think it presuming on our part, not of officials who would try to prevent it as illegal. You must not include me in the ranks of United Free officialdom : I was never in my life a member of any standing committee of Assembly, nor am I now, though I have tried to do my duty by the Church as a full private. If there are two men alive who have worked harder and more disinterestedly for it than you and Orr, I don't know them.

Our affairs at present look as black as can be, except inside the Church. I do not believe there is any prospect worth mentioning of discussion in our congregations ; but when it comes to negotiations with the other side, they have an unassailable position in the Lords' decision, and their only idea seems to be to use it unscrupulously, no matter what becomes of the work of the Church, to humiliate the majority and to rob them.　Isn't it queer to see a body which has just been fastened by the law to the Revolution Settlement recruiting the professors who are to train its ministers from O.S. and R.P. sources, whose *raison d'être* was and is to denounce the Revolution Settlement ?　But compared with other scandals, this is a scandal of a highly respectable character.

15 LILYBANK GARDENS, GLASGOW,
*December* 22, 1904.

Many thanks for your note.　If I write another book at all, I should like to write on a subject which needs a big one, and it could certainly not be done for next autumn.　Lately I wrote a paper on the Harnack and Loisy controversy about the Essence of Christianity : if you cared for that kind of thing for *The Expositor*—I think myself it is interesting, though I daresay it has gone off the boil for a little—I will send it. But I should have to abridge it somewhat.

Ramsay's new book [1] has a lot of interesting matter in it, mostly of the nature of preface to Revelation, or rather to the New Testament, and to early Christian history in general.　On the

---

[1] *Letters to the Seven Churches of Asia,* by Sir William M. Ramsay, D.C.L., LL.D.

epistles to the churches he has not any conclusive addition to make to what recent expositors have done.  I have written something about it in the *Magazine,* making the best of it, but hinting at the fantastic side of his new thoughts—which he himself admits.

I am glad to hear that you think the sale encouraging.  Until the booksellers return at the end of three months what they have not sold, I do not feel at liberty to be sanguine about this : Geddes is always sanguine, and requires to be discounted.  But it would be pleasant to think that more people were taking it.

15 LILYBANK GARDENS, GLASGOW,
*April* 11, 1905.

It occurred to me yesterday in sending you a notice of Rosadi's *Trial of Jesus,* that I never answered your last letter about the Commission. The reason was that the Commissioners decided at once not to hear the kind of evidence you and others were prepared to give, and that of course you knew at once.  On what principle they actually proceeded I could never make out, as they heard or refused to hear about the intentions of donors in the most capricious fashion.

I am going to America at the end of May, and will be away all summer.  The *Magazine* will be mainly in Dr. Orr's hands for the time, but I will

arrange for as much as I can before leaving ; and
will be able to have some hand in it all the time.
We do not hear much of it, and I have an impression that it is not taking hold to any great extent,
though the things that are said of it are friendly
enough.    We get very few books to review, fewer
than under the former conditions : why, I cannot
tell.    This, of course, is the dull season, but I
hope we may get more in autumn.

Do you think there is any opening in English
for a book of selections from Kierkegaard ?    I
do not ask as if I were intending to produce one
—I do not know Danish at all, but Dr. Grieve of
Greyfriars' here, the translator of Deissmann's
*Bible Studies*, and a really gifted man, knows
Kierkegaard well in his native tongue, and would
like to know whether there are prospects for such
a work.    I believe it would consist for the most
part of selections from his diaries, of which there
are eight volumes in print.    Amiel's journal is the
kind of model Dr. Grieve would have in view ;
but Kierkegaard is piquant and rebellious : not
apathetic and resigned.    I once thought of doing
a translation (from the German) of his extraordinary study of Abraham's sacrifice, and printing it in the *Magazine* as a specimen ; and I may
do so yet.    His more formal works do not seem
to me likely to have any vogue in this country.
They are as much eccentric as original, and with
sober minds a little paradox goes a long way.

What a preposterous book Rosadi's *Trial of Jesus* is! It is difficult to understand a man using such a subject as the vehicle for conveying his opinions on all that is of present interest in Italian politics ; but that is what he has done. As for the translator, if he knows Italian he does not know English, and his mangling of the ancient languages is past belief. Dr. Emil Reich, however, is the absurdest of the three, and ought to be put down. A man who knows himself to be infallible might surely be at the expense of good manners even in correcting fools, but this omniscient alien contrives to be as impertinent as he is absurd. He should be deported, and asked to apply his great mind to the relations of Hungary to Germanic Austria.

I was truly sorry for you that the Brighton election came just when it was most difficult for you to get the good of it, but it doesn't matter. Balfour is in to stay as long as the Septennial Act will let him, and all we can do is to wonder at the House of Commons which supports a man who so ostentatiously despises it.

15 LILYBANK GARDENS, GLASGOW,
*October* 4, 1905.

I only came back from America to-day, and was horrified to see in the *B. W.* opinions of mine about American preaching which I really

must disclaim. While I was on the other side
I heard very little preaching but my own ; and
B. has generalised from the impression I gave
him of one sermon I heard in ' the more cultured
part of the country.'   There are people preaching
in America, I dare say, as there are plenty
preaching at home, to whom it does not seem
to have occurred that Jesus is the Lord, and
that the Christian religion is faith, and that
faith is some kind of utter dependence ; and
the impression that kind of thing makes on
one who can read the New Testament is very
disconcerting.   But I never said or dreamt of
saying that that kind of thing was characteristic of American preaching, nor could I possibly
have any right to think or say so.   Do insert a
line to say that I disclaim any opinion about
American preaching, having only heard two or
three sermons during the four months I was in
the country.   I would not mind what anybody
represented me as saying except that everybody
in America was so kind to me, and this looks like
speaking ill of them behind their backs—and
makes me feel mean.

I enjoyed Northfield very much, especially as
I was staying with Paul Moody, who attended my
class here a couple of years ago, and who made me
feel at home.   Campbell Morgan was there, and I
heard him preach twice—once magnificently.
. . . It will not be news to you that the *B. W.*

has many interested readers both in the States and in Canada ; we came across them all over. We spent a fortnight before leaving for home in Canada, and saw Toronto, Montreal, and Quebec. They have done very well for Toronto in getting Kennedy and Kilpatrick to go there, and they have really a magnificent opening : I hope they may prosper. I have not yet seen any one here to know what our prospects are for the winter : we certainly will not have the Canadian support we had last year.

I hope you are well and fit for the winter's work : it does not seem politically as if it were going to be so short or so triumphant as some people expected a few months ago.

15 LILYBANK GARDENS, GLASGOW,
*October* 17, 1905.

Many thanks for the line you inserted about my opinion of American preaching : I only hope Bridgman will take note of it.

I have read Mackennal's life,[1] but except in a few sentences here and there it did not much interest me. The series of letters on which the author lays such stress is good enough, but the perplexities which it discusses are of the sort

[1] By the Rev. Dugald Macfadyen (James Clarke and Co.). The article to which Dr. Denney refers appeared as a signed leader in *British Weekly* of November 2, 1905.

which people generally digest in private. I have written a paper, not in connection with anything in the book, still less in America ; but apropos of a remark of Dr. Mackennal that he did not care much for the antithesis of objective and subjective in discussing the atonement. No more do I, and in fact what I have written is meant to show that the words in question are not only misleading but meaningless in any discourse about Christ. Of course I don't use them in the paper.

Our College opened to-day. Orr gave his lecture—one which he printed lately in an American Baptist Review—on 'The Place of Christ in Modern Thought.' Philosophers and historians seem always to be at cross purposes somewhat when they discuss this subject, but I never heard Orr so impressive and eloquent. I have no idea yet what kind of classes we may have, but we had the best meeting of former students we have had for a long time, and the air seemed to be rather more vital than usual.

You will see that the commission is getting under weigh, and I heard to-day from Howie that the latest rumour is that the minority will get either Aberdeen College or the Offices on the Mound. As you know, there are many in the Church, though more U.P.'s than F.C. men, who would quite cheerfully see Aberdeen thus disposed of. But as such a settlement would be equally resented by Aberdeen and by the Wee Frees, I should think it in the highest degree improbable.

I agree with you about the God save the people kind of hymn, and it may interest you to know that the commonest subject of complaint in our Churches, among old and young, men and women, especially those of any education, is that we have too few psalms in our praise and too many hymns. For this, organs are to blame.

15 LILYBANK GARDENS, GLASGOW,
*November* 8, 1905.

I send with this an article on Stevens.[1]  There is really just one mistake in the book, but it is perpetrated a thousand times, and makes him endlessly unjust to almost everybody he criticises : that one I think I have sufficiently pointed out.  I don't think I ever read such a *water-logged* sort of book ; it is really like one of the old wooden ships that would neither founder nor steer, and sometimes you feel as if there was not a soul on board to tell you even where they wanted to go.  His incapacity for seeing what earlier theologians were absorbed in when they discussed the work of Christ is astounding.  It has evidently been given (I should say)

[1] *The Christian Doctrine of Salvation,* by G. B. Stevens, Ph.D., D.D., LL.D. (T. and T. Clark).

as lectures to a class ; it is chopped into bits all of the same length no matter what the subject—the length being determined by the time at his disposal for lecturing purposes. The idea of his heading the anarchists in theology, considering his record, is too absurd.

Many thanks for the *Day-book of Claudius Clear*. I envy you everything in it—the abundance of matter, the ease or apparent ease of writing, the memory, the relevance, the good sense and good feeling—the whole thing, in short. I hope it may be as popular as its predecessor.

15 LILYBANK GARDENS, GLASGOW,
*November* 17, 1905.

Your reflections on professors interested me as they always do, and when the match is set to the gunpowder we will see what happens. I hardly think the explosion will be very alarming. If you add up the professors in all the colleges, the number who have gone to America or Australia in twenty years is not very great ; and though I have no intention of crossing the sea again, I don't suppose this kind of sin excites much animosity in the church. The root of all the evil is the length of the summer, and the *vis inertiæ* of men. I quite acknowledge that the Church pays for all my time, and I think, quite frankly, that it gets the whole

of my strength ; but I would be quite glad if
what it expected from me were more clearly
defined.  Here, in Glasgow, we all preach—all but
Lindsay, who has literally no breath ; and to
preach every Sunday all winter, even though you
only take one service, is a sensible addition to
your other work.  There are 200 churches in
Glasgow Presbytery, and it is only by the most
dogged rudeness to your co-presbyters that you
are able to keep out of week-night engagements.
I don't know how they do it in England, but here
it is quite impossible for professors as a class to
have nothing to do in Church work ;  you *must*
have to do with it, and let it pass as part of your
service, even though it is not favourable to writing
books or guiding thought.  The only remorseful
reflection that Orr, Smith, or I can have under
this head is that we have probably written more
books than had much guidance for thought in
them.  What did you mean when you wrote :
' I think I wrote you that I was hoping to hear
of the progress of the book ? '  What book ?
I am not writing one, though there is one wanted
on the Gospels ;  and I have foolishly undertaken
a number of articles both for Hastings and for
Jacobus (whom I liked better than any man I
met in America), that will take all my spare
time for a good while.  Some of them are on the
Gospels—I mean on Gospel subjects—and I hope
will be useful to those who read dictionaries.

What we really want here is a longer session, so much longer that we must be at our proper work most of the time; and that we shall not get. It may be lengthened by three weeks or a month, but no more, and even that is doubtful.

Orr is reviewing Stevens in the *Expository Times*. As he knows and likes him, he may be more complimentary to him than I.

15 LILYBANK GARDENS, GLASGOW,<br>
*December* 22, 1905.

I am sorry I cannot do a leader for you for January 4. It so happens that I have let myself in for a lot of things just at the holiday time, and will find it difficult to do this and to get the day or two off which I need.

I congratulate you on your 1000th number, and on the place the *B. W.* has attained. There was a young fellow in here last night who envied you the pontificate you exercised for such multitudes of readers in religion, politics, and letters. He put it in the disagreeable way of saying that he could not think of anybody who would be more missed than you, and told me he had read *The Iron Gate* with avidity by the light of the lamp on a country railway station. As his appetites are not particularly spiritual, this is an appreciation with which you have a right to be pleased.

One of the things which occupies a little of my time at present is reading the proofs of Lindsay's book on the Reformation which is coming out in Clark's International Series. Lindsay is one of the happy men who read a page at a time and therefore cannot spell; I am one of the poor wretches who do their reading in the infant school style, individualising vowels and consonants with scrupulous care, and therefore useful as a corrector of the press. I look forward to this when I can lecture no more. Lindsay's book, if I am any judge, is a really masterly piece of work, and it pierces me to the heart that it should come out in a series. There are to be two volumes, but they should have been published as an independent work; it would have been far greater glory both to Lindsay and the College, and the book would have had a far better chance of getting known as an authority.

15 LILYBANK GARDENS, GLASGOW, W.,
*January* 31, 1906.

I am glad you are going to have a rest, and will send something for the *B. W.* in time for the 15th. The election has dazed everybody a little, and politics will be more interesting than they have been for long when Parliament meets. You must feel rewarded for your efforts on the right side, and I hope the issue will not have anything in it to disappoint you.

It was very good of you to speak so cordially of the *U. F. C. Magazine* at the beginning of the month, and I fear it is not out of the need of it. The advertisements, which used to bring in a considerable sum, have practically vanished, and Geddes who has this in charge says he has so much other work to do for Hodder and Stoughton that he has simply no time to give to this.   If this is so, it is a pity, or, as an old gardener once said to me when I said it was a pity his strawberries had been blighted in a thunderstorm, ' It 's waur than a peety, it 's a loss.'   Envying your prospects of sunshine and profitable reading, in a Christian and Pickwickian sense, I am, &c.

BROUGHTY FERRY,
*June* 6, 1906.

I am truly sorry to refuse to help you just now, but it is really impossible.  My Communion address at the Assembly would be of no use, and this week is already congested with preaching and lecturing.

The Assembly was humdrum on the whole. I was not present at the Church and State discussion, as I had to leave that morning to be at a meeting in Shrewsbury.  The report in the *Scotsman* gave me the impression that there is

E

hardly more principle in our Assembly with regard to disestablishment than there is in the House of Commons with regard to religious education. If people get what they want themselves, they seem to find it enormously easy to forget others, especially if they are few. ' Why shouldn't Presbyterians combine in Scotland especially when their members would make other Christians a negligible quantity ? ' The certainty that other Christians *would* be treated as negligible greatly mitigates, I must confess, any enthusiasm I might feel for further union. I hope I believe in the mystical body, the body which is constituted by the one Spirit ; but in the visible reduction of this body to one legal corporation—and that is what our ecclesiastical unions produce—I believe less and less. Perhaps it is because I know Congregationalism less that I see or seem to see the truth in it but not its drawbacks. Anyhow, the drawbacks of a Church which has no external compulsion on it to be just are so conspicuous that I don't crave for more unions till we are all more conscientious men.

Have you any feeling that people are getting sick of the Education Bill, and that the Government will suffer neither for the goodness nor the badness but for the abhorred presence of the thing ? The only thing the ' silent voter ' wants is to hear no more about it, and if it were possible that it should lead to an election in spring, I fear it would be all up with the Liberal Government. The poor Government are much to be pitied when friends and foes conspire to prevent them from acting on principle, and then unite to denounce their unprincipled action. I am far from thinking you are to be pitied, but I am truly sorry that, after doing more than any other man to get a Liberal majority on this very subject, you should find your own principle of settlement the only one which meanwhile is declined all round. But the very impracticabilities of Clause 4 and all such clauses promise you success at last.

BROUGHTY FERRY,
*July* 2, 1906.

I am truly sorry to hear you have had so bad a time, and would have sent you something better if I could. But I have been here since the second week of April, and to add the business and the pleasures of one's old congregation for a whole summer to what had already been undertaken in the shape of other work has proved rather exhausting. My successor here, Macgilvray, has a year's leave of absence—he has been very ill—and I am on duty in his place till the beginning of September. If I had only had the church, it would have been delightful, but I had a good deal of other work on hand when I was asked what help I could give here, and, though you might not think it, I am really tired. However, as there is good news of Macgilvray, Mrs. Denney and I are enjoying the strange experience of resuming our old duties again and living in our old house.

I have been intending for some time to write to you about the Magazine : it does not seem to be doing at all. The advertisements have quite disappeared, and, as a large proportion of the revenue came from them, it can only be carried on at a heavy loss. At the Assembly too I heard from Geddes, who acts for Messrs. H. and S. in Edinburgh, that only 2300 were being printed, and that he had no idea of how many were being returned, as the returns were made to London. This seems to me just about as unsatisfactory as could be, and I really think it is worth while to consider whether in the circumstances it should be kept on. I know that neither Dr. Orr nor I would have anything to say if it were decided to discontinue it before the three years' experiment which you proposed to give it. It does not seem to meet any particular want in the Church, and it is difficult in a periodical which only comes out once in a month to keep up with the subjects of passing interest which might perhaps attract more readers. I have an impression too, though I do not wish to suggest that any one is to blame, that the disappearance of the advertisements is part of the result of a general want of interest in the commercial side of the business. But that may be quite wrong : one could understand that advertisers want a bigger circulation than the Magazine can claim. I wish you would tell me what you think about this, or what the publishers think.

What a jungle the Education Bill is becoming. If the House of Lords mangle it past recognition, do you suppose the present House of Commons would venture on the logical alternative supported by you and Chamberlain ? The more intricate the jungle, the clearer and more tempting the way out.

BROUGHTY FERRY,
*July* 26, 1906.

Many thanks for your letter. Should I write formally now to Messrs. Hodder and Stoughton about stopping the Magazine ? or is it enough that you have seen them about it ?

I have read the letters on the Sermon on the Mount with interest, and might write an article if it did not need to be a learned one.[1] I have not read Lyttelton's book, and as it is a big book I do not want to read it just now ; but if one could do anything relevant out of his own head I might try. When would you want it ?

As for ' my book ' and the ' solemn silence '

[1] These letters appeared in the *British Weekly* of July.

over it, I fear the silence must be maintained.
I do want to write something on the subject you
mentioned, and I even intend and hope to.  But
it will be a little while yet till I get started, and
even after that I may get stuck.  There is an old
Canon in *Consuelo*, who says it is much nicer to
talk about a book you are going to write than to
hear other people talking about a book you have
written ; but it is not this that makes me slow.  I
have a superstitious feeling that if I talk about
anything I will never do it at all.  No doubt that
damages in some way or other the things one does,
but I cannot get over the feeling that there is
something in it.

I hope there is nothing in what the specialist
told you about your lungs.  No men work more in
the dark than doctors, and cures seem to be due
either to nature or to faith—not to art.  I have
read most of Molière lately, and had some
happy times with his reflections on physicians.
The one thing I envy in what you have recently
betrayed of your prospects is the chance of talking
over a play of Shakespeare weekly with a competent person.  I should like to hear your con-
verse, and once in a while perhaps join in.

BROUGHTY FERRY,
*August* 7, 1906.

Many thanks for your letter.  I have written
to Hodder and Stoughton, and, as Dr. Orr had

already heard from them, I assume this is the end of the Magazine. I had told Dr. Orr what you said about the editing, so that there is no necessity for your writing ; but as his heart has really been engaged in the business not only while I have been his associate, but much longer, I am sure it would be grateful to him.

I am sending with this the article on the Sermon on the Mount,[1] and am glad you have a moralist like Dods and a critic like Moffatt to tackle it. But I am sure it was *meant* to defy the mind, which is a great part of the art of preaching, and that therefore nothing said by any or by all of us can either be or seem satisfying. It would be a great point gained if people would only consider that it *was* a sermon, and was *preached*, not an *act* which was *passed*. But these italics horrify me and I am sure you, so I will leave it here.

15 Lilybank Gardens, Glasgow, W.,<br>
September 15, 1906.

I am writing to ask a favour from you. On Tuesday I have to give the opening lecture at the Baptist College in Bristol, and if any one sends you a paragraph about it for the *B. W.* will you give directions to have it left out. The

---

[1] Dr. Denney's article on 'The Literal Interpretation of the Sermon on the Mount' appeared in the *British Weekly* of August 23, 1906.

reason I ask this is that I am going to give the same lecture at the opening of our own College next month, and if the heads of it appeared in the *B. W.* I should be given away. Are you going to the University celebrations at Aberdeen ? or do your notorious opinions about professors debar you from such functions ? A little of the kind of thing they are arranging will go a long way with most people.

The papers on the Sermon on the Mount seem to have provided lots of men with a text, but the general impression is that we are not further on. I had a letter of twelve pages from a Christian Socialist, accusing Dods and me of making conscience a higher authority than Christ. This is a ticklish point, but I answered him as discreetly as I could. Moffatt's article was the one I was most curious to see, and the one which did interest me most : it struck me as mighty clever, but so impalpable that only another man as clever as the writer would see all that was in it. He greatly relieved me also by writing two columns more than I did, for I was shocked to see that I had done one more than Dods. I expect we shall have him this winter at the Hall to deliver the Bruce lectures—the date, however, is not fixed.

Everybody here is sick of waiting for the Commission, and particularly disgusted that no settlement has yet been made about the New College.

The general impression, right or wrong, is that the fact of having the law on their side will eventually count to the Free Church for much more than it should; especially if any inference can be drawn from the attitude of the sub-commissioners. I only hope now that we may not lose our College as the price of saving the Edinburgh one, but this is an idea with which people's minds ought not to be familiarised.

BALLATER,
*October* 2, 1906.

I was sorry I did not have an opportunity of speaking to you at Aberdeen. Except at the banquet, I never so much as saw you, and though that, as it happened, was very much of a conversazione, we were hardly within conversing distance. I hope such a week of standing and smiling and speech-making may not take a year from the old Chancellor's life. On the whole, it was a much more imposing and successful function than the 450th anniversary of Glasgow, which was celebrated a few years ago.

I have thought over your proposal about the *B. W.*, and concluded to give it a trial. To be quite candid, I have no such fertility of mind as can be depended on to produce interesting matter regularly—I don't need to tell you that; but between books and other things I dare say

I might relieve you once a month, and it is a
pleasure to me to think that you have been
willing to ask me. If the circulation declines,
the remedy is obvious. The only condition I
wish to make is that you don't ask for anything
before November. The address I mean to give
in Glasgow would not make an article as it stands ;
it is far too long, for one thing ; but I dare say
I could get one out of it.

We have been staying here for a fortnight, but
leave at the end of the week, though I will not be
in Glasgow till the 12th. However, the Glasgow
address will always find me.

> 15 LILYBANK GARDENS, GLASGOW, W.,
> *November* 12, 1906.

The judgment was a great relief to us all :
and though our College will lose at least £25,000,
we neither lose our buildings nor our library, and
I quite agree with you that the Church is equal
to the situation. If the Free Church had evicted
*us* instead of the New College, I don't believe we
should ever have got back ; but they were too
anxious to wave the flag on the citadel, and now
Providence has got the better of them. The
audacity of ——, who says in their *Monthly*
that £100,000 will give their professors ' a living
wage,' but leave hardly anything for bursaries
for their poor students would be sublime if it
was not ridiculous.

Many thanks in particular for your own book. Do stick meanwhile to the outside ; I like the title and I like the cover : Mrs. Denney thought the cover ' humdrum,' but she was not in a happy humour at the time. I am going to read the preaching of Hall and Foster first, and then go through the rest again. Smith told me the other day he had heard some one at Mansfield preach a long and dull sermon on, ' Shall not the Judge of all the earth do right ? ' Do you remember Carlyle's indignation over hearing Hall preach once with his characteristic eloquence on ' God that cannot lie ' ? Things about preaching— not anecdotes only—interest me more than usually at present, as owing to Hislop's death I have two hours a week to take on Pastoral Theology.

15 LILYBANK GARDENS, GLASGOW, W.,
*December* 8, 1906.

I am posting with this an article on Oman.[1] He delivered these lectures in our College here, and I thought them exceedingly good. I think so still, though the exposition of his ideas is sometimes cumbered a little by unnecessary information, and sometimes by indifference and a kind of inarticulateness in himself. For those who can digest this kind of matter, however, it

---

[1] *The Problems of Faith and Freedom in the Last Two Centuries*, by John Oman, D.Ph. Leader appeared December 13, 1906.

is a very appetising book, and the more you
know of the people he writes about, the more
highly you think of it.

I am glad you like my articles in the *Dictionary*.[1] I rather grudged myself the time I spent
on them. Ramsay is always interesting, but I
happen to be one of the unfortunate people whom
he does not persuade, and if I were you I would
not lean too hard on him even though he *has*
taken his holidays in Iconium. He has got the
length now of referring to people who identify
the council of Acts xv. and the events of Gal. ii.
as a species of historical curiosities on whom no
more words are to be wasted ; but there must be
many people who have investigated this as
laboriously and patiently as he, and to whom it
is as certain as mathematics that this identification is correct. Harnack's book is certainly good
reading for those who have resisted what had
become a ' tradition ' of criticism ; it is even
amusing to see how Harnack raps everybody on
the knuckles for saying what he himself would
have said if he had written not very long ago ;
but Ramsay does not possess the art of sup-
pressing the personal equation so perfectly that
*he* should read *Lucas der Arzt* for the sake of
studying Harnack rather than Luke.

Did I tell you that this next week Moffatt is
coming to deliver his Bruce Lectures at the hall ?

---

[1] *Dictionary of Christ and the Gospels* (T. and T. Clark

The subject is St. Paul's Teaching on the Holy
Spirit. He is to be staying with us from Monday
till Thursday, and I hope to get better acquainted
with him.

15 LILYBANK GARDENS, GLASGOW,
*January* 17, 1907.

I am sorry you are not yet feeling up to the
mark, and will try to send something in time
for next week. But you seem quite vigorous,
and Providence is very good in providing you
with subjects. In spite of agreeing with what
you say about students and principals, we rejoice in a principal of phenomenal popularity
in the college and great influence in the Church,
who never preaches now : for better or worse
the rest of us are only too much in evidence in
that way. Our hall will not be like the same
place if Smith [1] goes to the University. None of
us would grudge his promotion, and he could do
a great deal to Christianise an institution which
is sure to become more and more influential, but
we should miss him more than words could tell.
I hope Carnegie Simpson will get Rainy's life to
write : he is immensely interested in it, and would
do it well.

[1] Dr. George Adam Smith, now Principal of Aberdeen University.

15 Lilybank Gardens, Glasgow,
*January* 19, 1907.

I enclose what was once a sermon : it has
not suffered transformation quite so well as I
expected, but it is the best I can do to-day.
Would you care to have an article on Creed
Revision, apropos of Mr. Templeton's book?
Some time ago Wallace[1] of the *Herald* asked
me to do one of the series appearing there
weekly, but I declined. Partly my mind was
not clear about what could be attempted, and
partly I felt that the Church could not think of
two things at once, and for some time to come
must be engrossed with other matters. But there
are aspects of the subject that are worth stating,
in view of what is in people's minds, and it might
turn out interesting.

The number of people who would like to be
Principal of Glasgow University is astonishing :
among those with whom I have any communication the betting is in favour of Jones. I should
say Smith comes next. The newspapers seem
to favour breaking the clerical tradition : but
what they want is an ' administrator,' and they
seem to take it for granted that they cannot get
this in a minister. I know them both very well,
and have no doubt that Smith would be a far
better man of business than Jones. He is be-

[1] Dr. William Wallace.

sides a far more thoroughly educated man,
except in philosophy.  Both would be immensely
popular with the students, and command far
greater interest in the community than has for
long attached to the post.  I hope your influenza
is as good as over.  My wife has had three months
bronchitis, with influenza in the middle of it,
which is pretty bad : but I remain unsympa-
thetically well.

15 Lilybank Gardens, Glasgow, W.,
*January* 29, 1907.

I was glad to hear you were going off to the
Riviera, although the proper place seems to be
Iceland.  On Sunday, and therefore on Monday,
I was in Edinburgh, and you know what a
Princes Street hurricane is ; I never saw such
weather, and I hope you may not see it in the
South.

The article on Campbell seemed to me pretty
decisive, and I don't know what more can be
said.  It is really not worth while to elucidate
any man's improvisations on God and the universe.  Setting conscience aside, as James Mozley
said, there are no two easier subjects to talk
about ; and pantheism just means setting conscience aside.  I do not believe there is any way
to argue against it except by insisting that conscience cannot be set aside—that it persists in

spite of all the systems which have explained it
away, and that a man knows quite well he is a
scoundrel when he applies solvents to it. Nothing
ever impressed me so much, as an argument for
theism, as the first verse of the 139th Psalm.
A man is incapable of judging anything if he does
not feel that it expresses the most real experience
of which human nature is capable. *Thou* hast
searched *me*, and known me—and if he does not
feel that the *thou* is just as real and as personal
as the *me*. Only God can prove His being and
His personality and His character to man, and He
proves all three, in the first instance, by experiences like this.

I believe I once quoted in *The Expositor* a thing
quoted by Sainte-Beuve in his *Port Royal* about
pantheism, which also impressed me much. It
was repeated to him, if I remember, by a friend
from a letter (no names were given), and was to
the effect that Christ has two great enemies, the
God Priapus and the God Pan ; and while you
can finally vanquish the former, you can never
quite get rid of the latter. The fascination there
is in the idea of a unity in which all differences
are lost must depend on some truth which the
mind hungers for ; but it is not easy to state it
in the right way. The answer in the Shorter
Catechism to the question 'What are the decrees
of God ? ' is one attempt to exhibit the truth, and
might be called an attempt to combine pantheism

with the personality of God. If the truth in this is questioned in the interests of morality, one is very apt to make man as independent as God, as if this were the only basis on which he could be regarded as responsible for his conduct. How to secure the intellectual formula which shall do justice at once to man's freedom and responsibility, and at the same time to his absolute dependence on God, is perhaps an insoluble problem ; but the latter truth, the one with pantheistic affinities, must have its due as well as the other. Goethe's airy saying about being a polytheist for artistic reasons, a pantheist as man of science, and a theist as a moral being, is a very good way of revealing the difficulties, but does not point at all to their solution. I often feel that Pantheism is akin to religions which make time and its contents unreal—like Brahmanism or Neo-platonism ; and in that respect at the antipodes of Christianity, in which history is the scene of divine works which have eternal meaning and value. The pantheistic temperament always feels strongly the relativity of all our knowledge and ideas, and indeed of all that ordinary minds call real, and it is characteristic of it in all those who know what it really means that Christ, like all historical persons, is brought under this law. He also pays tribute to His time. His person can have no absolute significance. There is no truth in Him which abides, and no work done by Him

F

which never loses its value. It is when it comes to be applied in this way that I am afraid of it, and I do not know any way to fight it but by appealing to Jesus Himself—especially to everything in Him which betrays or declares His sense of the absolute significance of His person and work, and especially also to the tremendous things He says about final judgment. Let a man be never so pantheistic, these things pierce to the dividing asunder of soul and spirit, and establish the great distinction at the vital point at which pantheism would fain have it annulled. But all this is commonplace, and I hope the opening of Parliament will relegate the New Theology to its proper place and spare the world the trouble of trying to understand a man who probably does not understand himself.

I hear no more about the Principalship,[1] but I have an impression that Smith's chances are improving. The Government, and at least Lloyd George, want Jones in Wales, and that is in Smith's favour. There is quite a strong citizen interest also on his behalf. . . .

I was in St. George's on Sunday, where there was great joy over Whyte's withdrawal of his resignation. They seem likely to call Kelman, and he seems likely to go. Yet they are conscious it will not continue their tradition.

[1] Of Glasgow University.

15 LILYBANK GARDENS, GLASGOW, W.,
*March* 5, 1907.

Many thanks for your kind letter, and for Lodge's book. I am rather interested in it as a whole than in the details, and will write something for next week. The book, I should think, is sure to be read eagerly by a great many people, and it probably represents a great quantity of mind *in* the Church, which has not been at the trouble of making its thoughts clear to itself. I wish it could be believed that all who are not of us were as thoroughly in sympathy with Christian ideas.

15 LILYBANK GARDENS, GLASGOW, W.,
*March* 9, 1907.

Here is what I have written about Lodge.[1] I once met him here and heard his lecture, and I like him very much. But though the spirit of his book is admirable, I cannot think this is the voice which is to lead many out of the wilderness. I have sometimes been tempted to say to my class that there are not many qualifications for preaching the Gospel of less value than second-class honours in philosophy, but after reading this catechism I begin to

[1] Sir Oliver Lodge published about this time a little book entitled, *The Substance of Faith allied with Science: a Catechism for Parents and Teachers*. A leading article on it appeared in the *British Weekly* for April 11, 1907.

be doubtful. It seems to me incredibly in-coherent in all it says about sin, and to have no power to discern things that differ. However, I have not gone into details about it : it is diffi-cult to do this when all the main questions are raised within a few pages. The great want of the book is any notion of epistemology. He talks as if to know how far it is from here to the Trongate or the moon, or to know that Lycidas is a fine poem, or to know that Cromwell was a heroic character, or to know that falsehood is a sin, or to know God, were all identical operations of the mind, and it leads to endless confusion. But I hope many people will read it, for I don't think it can do anybody harm, and there are no doubt those whom it will help.

I hope you are feeling better of your holiday. You have returned to this endless winter, I suppose ; here it is snowing as unconcernedly as if it were January. But I infer you are in good spirits from the story of the Socialist at the end of your letter in the *B. W.* It is the most com-forting story I have heard for a long time.

Possibly you are right in what you say about the views of Hegel and Cousin on God and Nature. The worst of it is that you cannot pin a pantheist down to anything. I suppose even Spinoza might have said that God ( = *natura naturans*) was, and was more than, nature ( = *natura naturata*) ; but it is just like saying that six (singly) is other, and therefore in some sense more, than half a dozen (=6 collectively). Lodge says at one place that God is ' a mode of regarding the universe,' at another that He is ' a part of the universe,' and at a third that He is ' a guiding and loving Father in whom all things consist.' It would be difficult to be fair or unfair if one tried to criticise this.

15 LILYBANK GARDENS, GLASGOW, W.,<br>
March 23, 1907.

Here is the other article. It was practically finished when I got your letter this morning, and though I have not appended any definitions, I hope it may serve your purpose well enough. I constantly felt in reading the book [1] that it was only a popular example of that Hegelianising of Christianity that was once so popular in Germany and is now extinct. In one way it can be represented as a systematic debasement of the Christian currency : every Christian term is used, but in a sense determined not by Christianity but by the philosophy : words like atonement, reconciliation, etc., being especially open to abuse. But though series of parallel definitions are an effective way of exhibiting this, the only thing certain about the definitions you give of your adversaries' terms is that they will

[1] *The New Theology,* by the Rev. R. J. Campbell, M.A. (Leader in *British Weekly,* March 28, 1907.)

dispute them; and without putting it exactly like this, I think what I have said will help even the simpler sort of intelligent reader to take up his proper attitude to the whole affair. I once thought of adding a paragraph about the Church and the Labour Movement, but decided not to. The article is already longer than usual, and I am not sure whether my criticism of this bit of Campbell would coincide with yours. Both intellectually and morally it seems to me as unsound as anything in the book.

What astonishes me much is how people with Bibles in their hands, and the great way of psalmists, prophets and apostles in thinking of these things before their eyes, can stand the puerility and the moral offensiveness of much of the New Theology. I have great faith that the Bible way of looking at everything human and divine will win in the long run, because it is the *big* way; and all uncorrupted minds succumb to that eventually. It is half-educated sophists who write New Theologies, deceiving and being deceived. You probably infer from this that I am glad to have done with them.

15 LILYBANK GARDENS, GLASGOW, W.,
*April* 1, 1907.

I was glad to see you meant to discuss the practical situation created by *The New*

*Theology.* For my own part, I cannot think it will be a serious situation very long. What strikes me most in looking back on the book is its extraordinary triviality compared with Scripture, and this is sure to be felt. I never preach to any kind of audience, in the poorest mission district, as I did last night, or in a well-off congregation, without feeling that the Church has the Bible in its heart far more than it gets credit for ; and a Church with this innate appreciation for Scripture will no more take the New Theology for Gospel than a man who knows Shakespeare and Milton by heart will take Davidson and Kipling for the greatest of poets. And to mention Davidson and Kipling is to put it too favourably for Campbell. However, there must be something to say ' for the present distress,' and I hope you may be guided to the right word.

I enclose short notices of two books you sent lately—one good of its kind, the other of a kind in which I find it impossible to get any joy. By all one can hear of it, Australia seems to be about the most godless place under heaven.

15 Lilybank Gardens, Glasgow, W.,
*April* 7, 1907.

I have rewritten and considerably expanded the last paragraph of the article on Lodge. In reality, I don't think I disagree with you, but on looking again at what I had said I became conscious of the missing links, and I think I have been able to supply them. In speaking of the grounds of faith in immortality it is necessary to remember that such faith did not originate with the resurrection of Jesus, however powerfully the resurrection reassured it : it was practically universal among the Jews of our Lord's time, and its roots in the experience of the Jewish Church will, I am very confident, be its roots always. To ask a proof of immortality which shall be independent of such experiences is like asking that Jesus should have manifested Himself not only to Mary and the Apostles, but to Pilate and Caiaphas—or to the Areopagus, perhaps, if we want a parallel to the Psychical Research people.

Do you know who wrote the ' Easter Sunday Reflections,' signed H. B. in this week's *Nation,* and the review of Dinsmore's book on *Atonement* in *Literature and Life* ?

Most people will agree with what you say about theological colleges making believers uncomfortable, but I am not sure that burning is the cure. I fancy it must be establishing a more intimate connection between them and the life and work of the Church, and this makes me doubt whether yon were right in giving such a cordial welcome to W. P. Paterson's proposals. The general tendency of these, however limited or qualified,

would be to make the divinity halls less part of the
Church—less under its influence and control, less
animated by its faith, life, and interests—and more
part of the universities.   Any one who knows the
university attitude to Christianity in this country
knows what that means.   Our whole situation is
terribly serious, and will become more so, but as
far as I see light in it, it is in the direction of the
Church taking more interest in its divinity schools,
seeing that they are used for *its* purposes, the
training of its members for its ministry, and not
for ends which are academic or scientific, perhaps,
but not the ends for which the Church exists.
There will have to be a great internal *éclair-
cissement* before there can be the effective co-
operation which is so desirable of the Church's
faith and the College's science in the training of
men for the Christian ministry.   The *Nation*
mentions this week that the students in the Protestant faculties of theology in the German
universities have fallen since 1871 from over
4000 to 2300, while the population of the Empire
has risen, I should think, in almost the reverse
proportion ;  and we are more nearly in the same
case than some people think.   There were more
students—a great many more—in our Glasgow
College when I entered in 1879 than there are now ;
yet then it was a Free Church College only, and
now it represents the United Church.   It is not
the College itself which is to blame for this ;  it

is the university and the general intellectual currents of the time. If there is no supernatural in any proper sense of the term—if even Jesus is only one more whose work could have been done by others had not He appeared—then there is no supernatural life in the world, and no room for an institution to guard or express it, and for an order of men whose vocation it is specially to represent it. The Church, if there is a Church at all, is not an institution in any sense, but the new moral and social order ; an official ministry is so far from being essential to it that it is a contradiction in terms of the true Christian idea. This is the state of mind we have to confront without becoming Catholics or legalists in religion. That the Catholics and legalists will gain in the coming crisis—I mean, get some gains—is probably inevitable ; but if we could get all the faith there is in the Church to apply itself intelligently to the situation I should not despair.

15 LILYBANK GARDENS, GLASGOW, W.,
*April* 13, 1907.

I hope you are too pessimistic about pantheism and morality. I always think it is men's excuses for their conduct that vary from age to age, not their conduct itself. Our passions, Montaigne says, are more constant than our reason, which is ' flexible à tout ' ; if men are going to be immoral they will be so, and if they have not pantheism as a plea they will have something else—or do without.  This sounds as fatalistic as if I were a pantheist, but I do not mean to speak of it lightly.  Somebody says that of all men of genius who ever lived Pascal was the least of a pantheist, and I have always felt this was just another way of saying he was the most of a Christian.

15 LILYBANK GARDENS, GLASGOW, W.,<br>
April 25, 1907.

The secretary of the Office-bearers' Union of our Church in Dundee has asked me to write to you and support an application of his that you should lecture to them, or give the opening address at their first meeting in autumn.  If you can do this, I need not say how much it would be appreciated.  You would get a very good audience—some cranks in it, no doubt, but many of the most loyal and devoted members of our Church.  I have done myself what they are asking you to do, and I do not think it would be wasting time, like addressing a Synod.

I have read Du Bose, and will write something about him, though there is nothing in his book that was not in his *Soteriology of the New Testament*, which I think I must have reviewed for you some fifteen years ago. The combination of effervescence and logic, or rather of effervescence and what is meant to be but is not logic, is not very attractive to me. But it is delightful in these times to meet a man who can write about St. Paul with enthusiasm, who believes that the apostle had a Gospel, and who rejoices himself to preach the same.

On the 15th of May I am going abroad for five weeks : I will be back on June 22nd. I don't want to do anything in the way of writing during that time, so if you have anything I could do for you before I start, you might let me know.

15 LILYBANK GARDENS, GLASGOW, W.,
*April* 28, 1907.

I post with this a short article on Du Bose's book.[1] The spirit and intention of it are very good, but his main idea is an exploded and antiquated one which only a mind that has lost its natural simplicity could stick to for so long. I have confined any criticism of the book to this central point, and have tried to be generous as well as just to him. I can hardly think that Sanday will accept his conception of the person and work of Christ without qualification, and, if he does not, there is nothing

[1] *The Gospel according to St. Paul*, by William Porcher du Bose, M.A.

else in the book to talk about. I forgive him much for his ardour for St. Paul.

15 LILYBANK GARDENS, GLASGOW, W.,<br>
*May* 10, 1907.

I enclose an article on Adams Brown's book. It is a very good book in a way, well meaning and free from objectionable qualities, mental or moral, but with a queer want of intellectual backbone about it. This, with what I sent on Du Bose, will ease your passage, I hope, over the next six weeks. We leave here on Wednesday first.

Watson's death is a terrible shock to all his friends,[1] and, though I only once exchanged words with him, I can understand from your article and otherwise how much he must be missed. His appointment at once to the Principalship at Cambridge and to the presidency of the Free Church Council would have given him new opportunities of proving the extraordinary variety and force of his gifts, and outsiders would have been eager to learn whether he could do anything to force English Free Churchmen into a homogeneous and effective force, political or religious. To judge by the way things are drifting in Parliament, a great deal of the fight for freedom is yet to come, or rather will have to be done over again.

[1] Dr. John Watson passed away in America in May 1907.

Campbell-Bannerman's words are strong, but the outcome as yet is not exhilarating.

Many thanks for the paragraph in your Claudius Clear letter about the people who write for books for bazaars, and who demand your favourite quotation and a shilling. The demand always paralyses me, and I have generally compromised by sending the shilling alone. I have never written my name on a book, but the man with whom I deal here must think me quite a devoted admirer of my own works. It gives me a shudder to think that he has paid 4s. 6d. for what may quite likely go at the end of the bazaar in the sixpenny or the twopenny box. If we had only the courage to strike!

I saw Carnegie Simpson's pamphlet in MS. and thought it exceedingly well done. It will serve a good purpose if it damps down a lot of the futile talk about union that is going on chiefly among people who don't care a penny for any religion or Church in the world, and others whose interest is obvious. Personally I have far more sympathy with Congregationalism than I think you have, or many Presbyterians; and I cannot get up the smallest enthusiasm over uniting all the Presbyterians and even all the Christians in Scotland in one vast legal corporation. The evils incident to the existence of such a corporation would be as vast as its benefits, or I am much mistaken; and I cannot think it was anything of

this kind that our Lord had in view when he
prayed that his disciples might be all one. What
we want for a while, anyhow, is not union, but
unity of spirit, and peace.

15 LILYBANK GARDENS, GLASGOW, W.,
*October 8, 1907.*

I was glad to hear from you again, and to
know you had enjoyed your holiday and had
good prospects for the winter. We had a very
pleasant time too, though we have been in
Glasgow since the 23rd of June, which is
a mistake. We were not in Germany but in
Venice and Switzerland, and for better or worse
I have no idea of the currents of thought there.
But I will send you an article in ten days or so,
if not on *Christus Futurus*,[1] which I have not
been able to look at, on something else.

Your suggestion about *The Expositor* bothers
me more. I have spent most of my time this
summer working at something which is connected
with your proposal, but in such a way that I am
rather hindered than helped so far as acceding
to your suggestion is concerned. What I have
in mind is like this. The Christian religion is
what it is, and what it has been all through its
history, in virtue of the place which Jesus holds
in it ; and the one question which really exer-

[1] *Christus Futurus*, by the author of *Pro Christo et Ecclesia.*

cises men's minds at the present time is whether
the place which the Church has given Him is one
which He Himself claimed : in other words,
whether there is a historical basis adequate to
support the spiritual phenomenon of Christianity.
I have done all the first part of it, showing *what*
the place assigned to Jesus in Christian faith has
always been : I have also done, what is an
essential part of the scheme, a statement of the
evidence for the Resurrection, in what seems to me
the proper form—in all, I dare say, 50 or 55,000
words ; but the part answering to your question
—What we know about Jesus—I have not yet
done. If nothing comes to hinder me, I count
on doing it next summer, and having it ready for
Christmas of 1908 ; but I could not undertake
a series of articles on it at the same time. Perhaps you remember my once saying that I had
a superstition—the opposite of your superstition
—about mentioning things I only intended to
do ; I would hardly have done it now except to
let you see that the particular suggestion you
made is a rather impracticable one at the moment.
Let us hope it will do no harm. I could more
easily give you an occasional expository paper,
but not a series. The last *Expositor* struck me as
particularly good, especially Mackintosh's paper,
but I don't know whether criticism like Bacon's
or mysticism like Macintyre's would soonest
make me hang myself. It *is* a particular kind of

' *mentalité*,' as Loisy says, which is represented in the Fourth Gospel, but lunacy is no kind of *mentalité* at all. If the Gospel consists of conundrums, which no one so much as guessed *were* conundrums till Bacon arose, the author deserved all the kinds of martyrdom that befell him.

15 LILYBANK GARDENS, GLASGOW, W.,
*November* 6, 1907.

With this I am posting a paper for *The Expositor*. The subject may seem threadbare, but I feel as if I had got the hang of it in a more morally intelligible way than some who have discussed it ; and if criticism, as you say, and not exposition, is popular at the present time, why, there is a little criticism in it too.

Forsyth's book [1] interested me very much, but the peculiarity of his style is such that only people who agree with him strongly are likely to read him through. It is immensely clever at some points at which it is not enough to be clever. It is like hitting Goliath between the eyes with a pebble which does not sink into his skull, but only makes him see clearer. When I went out last Thursday morning and saw the contents bill of the *B. W.* blazing across the street—' Dr. Forsyth replies to Dr. Denney '—it gave me quite a turn, for I was quite unconscious of having

[1] *Positive Preaching and Modern Mind,* by Rev. Principal Forsyth, D.D. (1907.)

G

said anything that called for reply. However, when I saw his letter I was relieved, and I have since had a very friendly communication from him. I hope his book will sell and be read, for it is needed, and, though some people will not be convinced, it should do a lot of good.

The article I wrote on Jesus and Paul was prompted by one of these *Volksbücher* which are having such a circulation just now. It is by Jülicher, and to be written by a professor of theology who prepared men for the ministry of the Christian Church is the most barefaced piece of paganism I have seen for many a day. It is called ' Paulus u. Jesus.'

The Principal, who has been off duty for a fortnight, expects to be back on Monday.

15 LILYBANK GARDENS, GLASGOW, W.,
*November 7, 1907.*

I wrote at the same time to you and Forsyth, and in both cases the letters crossed. It did not occur to me in writing on his book to say anything of the single sentence in which he refers to the bodily resurrection. I entirely agree with you that no relief is given by denying the bodily resurrection to any difficulty about the supernatural by any one who accepts *real* communications between a Saviour who survived death and His disciples, and that, short of such real communication, the Christianity of the New Testament has not a leg to stand on. But all this about evading the bodily resurrection is part of the widely diffused desire to get a religion free from historical uncertainty, and not dependent at any point on any testimony except the *testimonium internum Spiritus Sancti.* There is a good side to that; there is no saving faith but that which is spirit born and spirit attested, and people have the feeling that you cannot claim the witness of the spirit for any given story of the appearance of Jesus. What they do not seem to feel is that the whole phenomenon of Jesus (if one may use such an expression) crucified and risen, and seen and understood as it was seen and understood by the apostles, *is* attested by the spirit ; and that in this large sense there is an inward witness to the outward historical facts. If this were not so, I do not see how Christianity could survive. There are writers in plenty who do not seem to have the faintest perception of what the N. T. religion is, and of course such considerations are nothing to them. What do you think of this from Schmiedel ? ' The inmost religious good which I possess would not be injured at all if I had to admit the conviction to-day that Jesus never lived—as a historical inquirer, however, I can only say that of this I see no prospect.' What has a man who can say that in common with the man who says, ' The life that I now live in the flesh I live by faith in the Son of God ' ?   How it is to be cured I do not see, but the number of people who are on the slope that ends here, and who suppose that they are Christians while it is all the same to them if Christ had never lived, is appalling.   I have got rather weary of reading the kind of thing which Lake has done, as there is no new evidence and no new point of view for appreciating the old, but I will examine his book, and send a notice of it soon.   The merit of Forsyth is that he returns to his N. T.,—I delivered unto you *first of all* that Christ died for our sins.   I am as sure as I am of anything that people that stick at that will sooner or later come where Schmiedel has come, and I could forgive some rash *obiter dicta* to a man with whom I am so heartily at one on the main question.   He says ' the treatise ' is not for him, but if I were near him I would urge him to give up the policy of pinpricks and go in for a pitched battle.   If there were few to fight with him there would be plenty to cheer.

15 LILYBANK GARDENS, GLASGOW, W.,
*November* 14, 1907.

I enclose one or two reviews, including one, a little longer than so short a book usually gets, on Lake on the Resurrection.[1]   We have enough

[1] *The Historical Evidence for the Resurrection of Jesus Christ*, by Rev. Professor Kirsopp Lake.

and to spare of the kind of man who splits the
world into two unrelated sections called historical and spiritual, but mostly they do not quite
realise what they are doing. The odd thing in
Lake is that he has some perception of it, yet
does not seem to mind. ' To think that he
should know what he is, and be that he is '—it
is a spectacle, if not for men and angels, for philosophers and Christians to wonder at.

15 LILYBANK GARDENS, GLASGOW, W.,
*November* 29, 1907.

I will do something on Garvie [1] for next week.
I am glad you had another subject to propose,
for I was terribly disappointed with Illingworth.
He always seemed to me the ablest of the *Lux
Mundi* men, and I have read all his works with
profit, but this book on the Trinity [2] is obscu-
rantist and irrelevant to an incredible degree.
I have written as polite a notice of it as I could,
but it is impossible to praise anything in it which
is related to the subject.

15 LILYBANK GARDENS, GLASGOW, W.,
*December* 16, 1907.

The best thing I could do with this article
was to omit the references to Demonology and

[1] *Studies in the Inner Life of Jesus*, by Rev. Principal Alfred E.
Garvie, D.D.

[2] *The Doctrine of the Trinity Apologetically considered*, by Rev. J. R.
Illingworth, D.D.

the Second Advent, and to replace them by a
shorter paragraph on the general subject of our
Lord's knowledge. I am very sensible of the
difficulties connected with both subjects, and
perhaps do not estimate them quite as you do.
I have thought of all the things you say before
as well as since your writing them, and am
prepared to leave more room for agnosticism.
The only thing that makes me hesitate in the
least to give up Demonology is not the authority
of Jesus, which I cannot use exactly as you
seem to do, but the fact that I have known a
saintly person, pure, affectionate and charitable
in a signal degree, on being deprived of reason
become in every respect the opposite—foul,
malignant, and unspeakably restless and miserable. The unknown quantity in this is bad
enough to be the devil or his angels.   The Second
Advent is far more important, but it is not only
true as you say that the Epistles are pervaded by
the glow of it, but that in the form in which the
writers of the Epistles expected it, it has never
been fulfilled.   There was an error of some sort
or at some point in their hope.   I do not like to
say that our Lord was responsible for it, though
I do not doubt that the hope in general is to be
referred to Him.   Is it not possible that words
like those in Matthew and Luke—*From henceforth* ye shall see the Son of Man *sitting* on the
right hand of power and *coming* on the clouds of

heaven—suggest a continuous rather than an instantaneous advent, something to which the experience of Pentecost rather than of the Last Day are the key ?   Of course there are the sayings on the other hand about the lightning flashing in an instant from East to West : but that is just the difficulty—there *are* two sorts of sayings referring to the same thing, and there is the commentary of experience to throw into the scale, for the one and against the other.   It is rather curious that half the readers of the N. T. should cling to the Second Advent in order to maintain the authority of Jesus, while the other half is asserting and emphasising the very same apocalyptic passages with a view to undermining His authority.   There is something here to be cleared up, and I thought Sanday's point—that apocalyptic language is used by Jesus in other connections, not literally, but in a symbolical sense—an interesting one and worth mention.   However, I have no desire to disturb any one's hope, and I think you will find what I have written unobjectionable, and perhaps not quite pointless.

15 LILYBANK GARDENS, GLASGOW, W.,
*December* 31, 1907.

I am very sorry you are laid up again; I hope it will not be a severe attack.   When you wired, I had gone to Blairgowrie to the funeral of an old class fellow, Osborne of Dundee; and in the congested state of the lines I did not get home, nor your message, till near midnight on Saturday. Yesterday I had to preach. I mention all this that you may see I have no qualification for writing about Rainy except that I have not influenza. If I had had a little longer, I dare say it would have been a little shorter, but you can remedy that and anything else in it as you please. Excuse the haste of this as I am just going out to the post.

15 LILYBANK GARDENS, GLASGOW,
*January* 13, 1908.

It was very kind of you to write to me as you did, and I ought to have acknowledged it sooner.[1] But you can understand. We had been married for more than twenty-one years, and in all that time I never had a thought of which my wife was not part, and I hardly know yet what has befallen me. I have no doubt you are right in bidding me work, and I am sure nothing could grieve her more than if I were to be faithless for her sake to any of the persons or causes in which we used to take responsibility together. But it came so suddenly that I was stunned for a while, and though I did what had to be done it was in a kind of dream. Happily I am not alone just now, having my wife's sister

[1] Mrs. Denney died in January 1908.

with me, a sister of whom we were both very fond, and with whom I can speak of her as freely and as intimately as I wish. I cannot be sufficiently grateful that she was with her when she was taken ill. They had been shopping together on the Saturday afternoon, and literally the last thing my dear wife did in this world was to order a set of books as a Christmas present for me. It was rather expensive, but she said to her sister as they left the shop she was so glad she had got it, for she knew the surprise it would be to me and the pleasure I would get out of it. They were crossing from the bookseller's to the subway to come home when she was stricken with a violent pain in the head and sickness. A girl passing fetched a cab, and when she came home she could walk upstairs. The doctor thought it was a violent attack of influenza, and, when we told him we had meant to go to Moffat at the end of the week, assured us there would be no difficulty about that. She was very prostrate for three days, but quite clear in her mind and, except for the headache, which continued, quite cheerful. In point of fact, it was a slight hæmorrhage on the brain, which recurred in a severer form at ten on Wednesday night. She became unconscious immediately, and in three hours was dead. We did not know she was dying, and said no good-bye. Yet the last word I had said to her was adieu, and she waved her hand feebly, and gave me the look she always did when I went out to my work. It seemed as though I never could work any more without it, and yet I feel now as though I never shall be without it, and I must resolve even for her sake not to be faithless, but believing, and do what I can. You will forgive me for telling you all this : though you never saw much of my wife, you have been so constant a friend to me that I am sure you will understand.

I was very much interested in all you wrote about your father, and could have wished to know him. His love for the classics and especially for Horace attracted me. An evangelical Christian who appreciates Horace deserves Horace's *Omne tulit punctum* better than any kind of man I know. Once in the *Union Magazine* I wrote a line or two about your Letters on Life with just this allusion to Horace in it, but I was not aware that your appreciation of the Horatian as well as the Pauline view of life was inherited. When they are separated, in ordinary mortals, Paulinism is feverish and Horace insipid ; but it does me good to think of a solitary scholar who got the full good of both.

I am sending with this an article on Gore's book.[1] It is a hurried book, and with no kind of unity, yet here and there it has interesting

[1] *The New Theology and the Old Religion,* by Charles Gore, D.D., D.C.L., at that time Bishop of Birmingham.

points.  There is something picturesque in the
meeting in one city of two such worthy representatives of the scientific and the Christian intelligence of our time as he and Sir Oliver Lodge :
it should make the negotiations or the controversies of science and theology worth following
in their neighbourhood.  But it is the more a
pity that reference has to be made to Campbell
and the New Theology.  He is not on the level
of dignity and manners which belongs to the
Bishop and the Principal of the University.
Perhaps you may not agree with what I have said
about Gore's ideas of ' massing ' the opinion of
the artisans in the Church.  It strikes me there
is a lot of unsound talking about this, and, what
is worse, a lot of unconscious patronage.  My
father was a working man, and while no man
could have been freer from any kind of self-
assertion, I am certain it would have seemed very
queer to him to be regarded *in the Church* as
belonging to a particular class which had to be
recognised in some particular way.  With all
our faults, the self-respecting working man can
keep his self-respect, and be at home in our
Church as completely, I believe, as in the apostolic age.  I had rich merchants, secretaries of
financial companies, schoolmasters, shopkeepers,
tradesmen, and coachmen in my session, and we
were as true a brotherhood in Christ as a minister
could wish to have part in.  There is no need that

a different degree of education should separate
men, and I am quite certain that decent working
people are proud to think their minister is a
thoroughly equipped man, and like him the better
and not the worse for it.

15 LILYBANK GARDENS, GLASGOW,<br>
February 4, 1908.

I am sending with this the article for *The
Expositor* on 'The Cup of the Lord and the Cup
of Demons.' If you want or need to curtail
it any, the easiest way would be to omit the
last two pages, beginning at 'The lesson of this
passage,' on p. 14. But I hope you need not,
as it is not over the usual length, I think, and
I am interested in the lesson.

I am curious to know what you cannot assimilate in my article on 'Preaching Christ.' It is
so long since I wrote it now that I have only a
general recollection of it, but I hope you agree in
the main. I rather regretted giving it to Hastings,
for there are some things in it I want to put into
the book I have in mind, but I daresay he may
not object to this. Judging by your review and
by some conversation I had with Dr. Orr, who is
reviewing it for the *Scottish Review*, the new volume
seems miscellaneous and inconsistent in a high
degree. Dr. Orr says there are eleven or twelve
places in it where the census under Cyrenius is

fully discussed, the same evidence adduced, and all sorts of incompatible conclusions announced.

I have had a week to-day of living here absolutely alone, except for people coming in, of which I have had enough. There is nothing to do but work, and every inducement except the one which once made every other needless.

I hope you and all your house are well.

15 LILYBANK GARDENS, GLASGOW,
*March* 17, 1908.

Many thanks for your letter and your kind thoughts of me. I think I understand Calvin's saying, and am happy, I am sure, in having at least one person who loved my wife so truly that I can speak of her almost as unreservedly as I think. Smith, too, has been the kindest and truest of friends ; he really knew and appreciated her, and the notice he wrote of her for you was grateful to her sisters as to me. These bright spring days I have seemed to miss her more than ever : she had the keenest delight in all the sights and sound of spring, and the blackbirds in the park in the morning literally infected her with their own exhilaration. It is another life to hear them alone. I hope you are better than when you wrote. We have had much influenza and other illness here too, yet the winter was not severe.

I have been reading Loisy, and will write something about him soon. As bad luck would have it, I had spent 24s. on him myself and sampled him freely before your copy came. Shall I return it, or present it in your name to the Library, which is sore smitten by the Wee Frees? If you happen to have his book on the Encyclical, I should be glad to have a look at that. There is an interesting letter on it in the *Spectator* this week by a R.C., and though the writer (and Loisy too) disown all philosophy and *Apriorismus*, I feel sure it is the philosophy of this whole business — its preliminary assumptions and its view of Christianity as a whole—which needs to be considered. There is no use in dividing the Gospel into 140 paragraphs, and criticising them on the principle that no chain is stronger than its weakest link. This metaphorical argument is sufficiently countered by changing the metaphor, and saying that the statue as a whole carries conviction though you may be puzzled by a chip. What strikes me on the whole about Loisy is that there is no continuity, on his showing, between Jesus and the Christian religion. He did not originate it either directly or indirectly. He lived and died under an illusion or delusion which L. does not hesitate to call *naïf* and *absurde*, and it was not out of any revelation made in him or by him, or out of any great conviction he held, but apparently in getting the better (in-

consistently enough) of his naive absurdities
that the Christian religion made its way in the
world. The Gospel—that is, the religion of
Jesus—was a dream; but it died; and only
when it died was Christianity born. I don't
wonder the Pope excommunicated him, but only
that he left it to the Pope to do.

15 LILYBANK GARDENS, GLASGOW,
*March* 28, 1908.

I have written something on Loisy,[1] and send
it with this. The only remarkable thing about
his book is its appearance in the Church of
Rome. The air of 'preternatural suspicion' in
which he criticises everything in the Gospels is
remarkable too, and sometimes one remembers
gratefully the saying, 'Whoso speaketh a word
against the Son of Man it shall be forgiven
him.' I never had any difficulty about the clause
in our confession that calls the Pope Antichrist,
but in this present case I am quite on the side
of the Church. If the members of the Church
read this book and believed it, there would not
be two or three left in the world to meet in the
name of Jesus. Still, the human mind is capable
of the queerest inconsistencies and perversities,

---

[1] A signed article by Professor Denney on M. Loisy's work on the
Synoptic Gospels appeared in the *British Weekly* of April 9, 1908.
The title is 'Taking away the Lord.'

and except for impenitent vice of some kind one always has misgivings about excommunication.

I have been reading your articles on Socialism with great interest.[1] It is not a subject on which I have any scientific opinions, but I cannot say I could make out any ground for distinguishing between property which would and would not, or could or could not, be socialised. It seems to me that all the property I have is of one kind. If I lend my savings to the Corporation of Glasgow and they put them into the Tramway system, they have no more right to the dividends they promised to pay me on them than they would have to my plate and spoons, suppose I had invested them thus, or to my old wines or first folio Shakespeares if I had bestowed them so. Property is that with which a man can do pretty much as he will, and if property ceases too in capital, the only quite certain result (I should say) is that capital itself will soon cease. If individuals don't save, Society will not, and capital will presently disappear. Probably your studies will make this seem nonsensical to you, but so it strikes me. I am not afraid of Socialism, though foolish experiments may be made by a combination of the benevolent and the bad, but when it comes to the point, the people who have anything will astonish the people who want just to take it from them. Winston Churchill in a speech he

[1] *The New Socialism: an Impartial Inquiry*, by Jane T. Stoddart.

once made here in Glasgow indicated very sagaciously the point at which the seemingly swift and irresistible growth of Socialism would meet a check.

15 LILYBANK GARDENS, GLASGOW,<br>
April 3, 1908.

I am going for a fortnight to Moffat on Monday with my brother and sister : if you want to send me a proof of the article on Loisy, please have it addressed c/o Henderson, Mayfield, Moffat. After the 20th, I shall be at home again.

Enclosed you will find the article for *Expositor* on 'Coming by water and blood.' I did it now, partly because I had the chance, partly because it touches on the sacraments, as the one I did last month also does, and it might be as well not to have them too far apart. But if you think differently it will do for a later number.

It is difficult here to follow the Bp. of St. Asaph and Mr. McKenna, or to know whether there are personalities as well as principles influencing different members of the Government, as is freely asserted. Your earnest appeal has all the logic and all the facts on its side, but it is a desperate business to have to do with men who pride themselves on not being logical, and shut their eyes to facts. I have more hope of the

H

Government on Temperance than on Education, for they have a better chance of a fair fight. If it only continues furious enough it may put education into the background, and the number of people who are getting sick of attempts to satisfy all the Churches by compromises, which *ex hypothesi* must fully satisfy none, will make this all the easier.

15 LILYBANK GARDENS, GLASGOW,
*May* 7, 1908.

I will be very glad to write something on Smith,[1] especially when I may let the archæology alone. It is not in my line in the least. He showed me the New Testament sheets of his book, and, like you, I was much impressed by the part about Christ, and in particular by Smith's sense of the difference between Christ's way of speaking and that of the prophets. Of course a man who cannot see this is stone blind in the Bible, but it delighted me to see how deeply Smith had been impressed by it, and I twice spoke about it in my class last session. I am basing much on it in the book I am trying to write, as justifying the whole attitude of N. T. faith to Jesus.

I finished Adam's[2] book last night, but cannot

---

[1] The reference is to Sir George Adam Smith's work on *Jerusalem*. (Leader in *British Weekly* of May 28, 1908.)

[2] *The Religious Teachers of Greece*, by James Adam; edited, with a Memoir, by his wife.

write anything about it till next week. Some
of it seems to me extraordinarily good, but I
know what you mean when you call it disappointing. What ought to have been the best and
weightiest bits in it are not so, and with all the
zest and fervour there is a certain want of composure and weight. He seems to have known
rather little, too, outside of his historical beat :
his only Christian teachers are Hastings' *Dictionary* and Matthew Arnold. But in a race
such as his life seems to have been against death
and time, the imperfections rather call for com-
passion than comment, and I don't know in
English nearly so useful a book of its kind.

15 LILYBANK GARDENS, GLASGOW,
*May* 22, 1908.

I might have sent the enclosed last night
and saved you the trouble of wiring. The book
is a really admirable companion to the Old
Testament, and though not every part of it
can be equally interesting to every one, it is
a remarkable proof of the manysidedness of
Smith's own interest that he has done every
part of it with such thoroughness. The book
I am trying to write is really an elaboration of
the argument in his chapter on 'The Temple
and the Lord.' I have got on a good way, and

though there are a lot of interruptions ahead I hope to have it finished by the beginning of the session.

About your proposed *Aids to Faith* I have no suggestions meanwhile. I have seen a number of the German series to which you refer, but do not think them likely to be of much use here. The paper and the type are unattractive, and in some cases the style and temper are equally so. There seems to be less of sweet reasonableness in the Fatherland than in less scientific countries, and I am quite sure you are right in aiming at native rather than foreign productions. If the other thing were once off my hands I would gladly try once more to say in the briefest and most persuasive way what I have to say about the atonement and the forgiveness of sins, but I cannot undertake it till then. *The* thing that is wanted to keep people from lapsing into Unitarianism—which has all the science and all the philosophy in the universities on its side—is a tract on the lines of that chapter of Smith's, showing that the attitude of New Testament Christianity to Jesus is justified and demanded by Jesus' consciousness of Himself. This is to be the burden of my book, but it might be condensed and brought to a practical issue in such a series as you have in view. But I must do the book first. Another thing wanted is a little book on the sources for the life of Jesus. But I have

not had time to think round the field, and will
write you again when I have done so.

15 LILYBANK GARDENS, GLASGOW,
*July* 2, 1908.

I send with this a paper for *The Expositor* on
Jesus' estimate of John the Baptist : perhaps it
might better be called simply ' Jesus and John
the Baptist.' Also a notice of Du Bose's last
book which you sent me.

I am going to preach in Interlaken from
July 19 to August 16, and expect to leave here
this day week. What address I may have there
I cannot tell, but if you wish this paper in the
August *Expositor* the proof would either need to
be sent here before I leave, or forwarded there.
I expect to be there on the 17th, and I suppose
' Scotch Church ' would find me.

The heat here is tremendous, and I hope it
may be past the worst before I have to start.
Interlaken itself is a hot enough place without
any aggravations.

I have a note to-day from Hodder and Stoughton
wanting a description of my book to advertise
it in the colonies. What occurred to me as a
title, when Mr. Stoughton was here, was ' Jesus
and the Gospel,' but I am not just satisfied with
that. The idea I have is to show that the Gospel,
as the apostles preached and believed it, can be

verified in the mind of Jesus. There is something
known to history and experience as Christianity
—something of which the New Testament is the
classical example—and I want to prove that those
who accept it are not false to Jesus, but true to
Him; or, in other words, that the historical
Jesus supports and not discredits the Gospel.
If you can think of anything better for a name it
will be a great obligation to let me know.

15 LILYBANK GARDENS, GLASGOW,
*October* 9, 1908.

I enclose a short notice of Forsyth's book,[1]
which I found very difficult to read. If this
is how one feels who is heartily at one with
the writer, how must it strike an unsympathetic
reader ? He has more true and important
things to say, in my opinion, than any one
at present writing on theology ; but if these
papers were preached, as most of them seem to
have been, I am sure most of the audiences, while
willing enough to take hold of them, must have
been sadly perplexed to find the handle. To convince a man that he has an inadequate or false
view of the Gospel may do him good, or rather
must do so ; but to give him a strong impression
that you are contemptuous of his view of the
Gospel while you do not enable him convincingly

[1] *Missions in State and Church*, by P. T. Forsyth, D.D.

to apprehend the better one may have quite opposite effects.   But I do not like to say these things about a man whom I like so much, and in the few lines I have written I do not do more than allude to them.

I was sorry to see from the *B. W.* a while ago what a rainy holiday you had in Aberdeenshire. We had a delightful month in Switzerland.   My sister-in-law came with me, and, though we travelled little, we had such weather that I think we were able to be in the open air an average of eight or nine hours daily.   I was very much the better of it, and hope to get through the winter well, though I have already promised to preach once every Sunday except at the Christmas holidays. . . .

We begin again at the hall on Wednesday.   Orr is to give the opening lecture, but he has not yet announced his subject.   Smith is on tour in England, having a great time.   If you have any ideas on the tenure of the pastorate I should be much your debtor for them, having been appointed convener of a committee to report on this to the Assembly.

15 LILYBANK GARDENS, GLASGOW,
*November* 21, 1908.

I enclose one or two reviews.   Ferrero's book on Rome and Egypt [1] is one of the

---

[1] *The Greatness and Decline of Rome*, vol. iv., ' Rome and Egypt,' by Guglielmo Ferrero.

most vivid and interesting books I have ever read; I could not have believed it possible that on such a well-worn bit of the field any one should have made such a brilliant display. The other books are not much worth. Warschauer's [1] is the abler of the two, though I don't think he realises how much he has thrown away, and how greatly he deceives himself by verbal association about the worth of what he keeps; the other man, Nolloth, [2] has a fair acquaintance with critical opinions on the Gospels; but though he writes of 'The Person of our Lord and Recent Thought' he has not so much as begun to think. Judging by the Claudius Clear letters your vitality has not been impaired in the least by your visit to the North. I hope you may keep it up through the winter. Since you were here we have enrolled a few more men at College, and for the first time for some years have touched 100. I wish I could be convinced that more men were entering the Church, not the ministry: if we get members, the ministers will be all right.

GLASGOW, 15 LILYBANK GARDENS,
*December 7, 1908.*

Your letter was very reassuring and grateful to me, and I am happy to think that the

[1] *Jesus: Seven Questions*, by J. Warschauer, D.Phil.
[2] *The Person of our Lord and Recent Thought*, by Charles Frederick Nolloth.

argument of my book as a whole commands your assent. This is really what I am interested in, and though I am prepared to stand by critical details of various kinds, I am also prepared to find that they do not convince every one. As for your remark that you missed an unequivocal statement that Jesus is God, I feel inclined to say that such a statement seems unattractive to me just because it is impossible to make it unequivocal. It is not the true way to say a true thing. I think I have made it plain that for me to worship Jesus as God is worshipped, to trust Him as God is trusted, to owe to Him what we can owe to God alone, is the essence of Christianity : I have said in so many words that no one means what a Christian means by ' God ' unless he includes in that all that a Christian means by ' Father, Son and Spirit.' This I hold to be the Catholic doctrine of the Trinity, but I dread ways of putting it which do nothing but challenge contradiction. ' Jesus is God ' seems to me one of these provocative ways, and therefore I avoid it. It has the same objectionableness in my mind as calling Mary the mother of God. The N. T. says θεὸς ἦν ὁ λόγος, but it does not say ὁ λόγος ἦν ὁ θεός, and it is this last which is really suggested to the English mind by Jesus is God. Last week the Rev. Dawson Walker, D.D., theological tutor at Durham, sent me a penny book on the Trinity he has written for

Church of England young men. He takes this (as I think) mistaken line: ' Jesus Himself claimed to be God,' etc. I can only say that the wrong things it suggests seem to me so completely to outbalance the right that we can well afford to dispense with it.

About the Creed, I did not make in my mind any distinction between members of the Church and officebearers in it. On general grounds I think the less distinction there is made between the members of Christ and their obligations, theological or moral, the better; though it is arguable, no doubt, that once there is an organised Church those who represent it officially should be more completely than others in harmony with the average theological opinion. Nevertheless, I am inclined to think that the dangers of legalism here are greater than those of liberty.

About reviewing it in the *B. W.* I have really no useful suggestion. I should value your own mind upon it, to say the least, as much as that of any of the men you mention ; and apart from some ' critical ' questions in the second book, it is not specially ' expert ' qualifications that are required for its appreciation. I should rather know how it appealed to the average educated members of the United Free Church than to Moffatt or Forsyth—and especially to those who are under forty. I sent Moffatt one, and he has promised me his serious thoughts later. The only other name which occurred to me was that of Cairns in Aberdeen.   It is a line in which he is interested, but whether he would write the kind of thing you require I do not know.   I don't wish you to do it against your will, or if you feel it irksome or think it in any way inexpedient ; but I should rather you did it than anybody else. It is quite possible that Forsyth or Moffatt may do it elsewhere.

I was delighted to hear you were beginning your literary history and on such a scale.   Six volumes of 150,000 words stagger the ordinary idle worker, and I can only say *Macte virtute esto*.   Though I have several times spoken of Chalmers, I have no essay on him at all : only a distinct impression that he is our greatest man since Knox, and greater than all his works.   He had the greatness of the nation in him as well as that of the Church, and it is an immense gain to a Churchman when he has such an interest in the State as keeps his ethics from becoming ecclesiastically narrow in range.   If I can be of the least service to you at any point I shall be delighted.   I will write soon about Church and Kingdom, but my class is waiting.

15 Lilybank Gardens, Glasgow,
*December* 12, 1908.

It was very kind of you to write to me again, and I really do not think there is any difference between us. When you say that you do from your heart believe that God was manifest in the flesh, I am sure I can say the same. I have often said in teaching that if a man does not worship Christ I do not care what he thinks of Him—he does not see what is there; and I have missed the mark completely in what I have written if I have not made it clear that all men should honour the Son even as they honour the Father. Probably the aversion I have to such an expression as Jesus is God is linguistic as much as theological. We are so thoroughly monotheistic now that the word God, to put it pedantically, has ceased to be an appellative and become a proper noun : it *identifies* the being to whom it is applied so that it can be used as the subject of a sentence ; but it does not unfold the nature of that being so that it could be used as the predicate in a sentence. In Greek, and in the first century, it was quite different. You could say then ὁ Ἰησοῦς θεός ἐστιν. But the English equivalent of that is not Jesus is God (with a capital G), but, I say it as a believer in His true deity, Jesus is god (with a small g—not *a* god, but a being in whom is the nature which belongs to the one God). I have no objection at all to Parker's formula, Jesus is God the Son, because ' the Son ' introduces the very qualification of God which makes it possible to apply it to Jesus. In the same way I have no hesitation in saying

Jesus was God *manifest in the flesh,* because 'manifest in the flesh,' serves the same purpose. It is because God is to all intents a proper noun with us, which, if it is used as a predicate at all, must make an equation with the subject (Jesus is God being the same thing as Jesus=God), that it seems not only to me, but I am sure to most people, an unnatural way of declaring their faith in Christ as Immanuel—God with us. Jesus is man as well as God, in some way therefore both less and more than God; and consequently a form of proposition which in our idiom suggests inevitably the precise equivalence of Jesus and God does some kind of injustice to the truth. Forgive me for being so expository on this, but I don't want you to think that I have other than the highest thoughts of our Lord and Saviour. I wrote my book for nothing so much as to assert for Him, in a way which would perhaps appeal to some people afresh, the name which is above every name : there is nothing I say more fervently than To Him be glory for ever.

I am sorry I don't know much of the English history to which you refer. Fairbairn's appendix to Dorner is very appreciative of Doddridge, and I don't want to think ill of the man who wrote ' When I survey the wondrous cross.' About Watts he mentions some writings of his later years which not only his orthodox executors, but Lardner, who was a Unitarian, thought unfit for publication; Fairbairn apparently believes that his mind had given way; and that his Unitarian views are the incoherent scribblings of his dotage. This is surely not the posthumous work to which you refer ? I will try to acquaint myself better with the story, but I confess I find the kind of thing very irksome. The very idea of historical interpretation was either lost or had never been properly discovered when Clarke and Waterland controverted one another, or Priestley and Horsley : I do not feel when I read in them that one is right and the other wrong, but that we have sailed into other latitudes, and that the whole relation of the mind—I mean the believing Christian mind, loyal to Christ—to questions of this kind is different. Our whole conception of revelation and of scripture has changed. No doctrine is for us *merely* a question of exegesis, and though I think most heresies would have been nipped in the bud if men had been able to parse, we must take the mind as it is, and speak to it for Christ as we can. I have no opinion of whether I have done well, but I am sure I meant well.

15 LILYBANK GARDENS, GLASGOW,
*January 9, 1909.*

I cannot thank you enough for your far too generous appreciation of my book.[1] It

---

[1] A leader on Dr. Denney's work, *Jesus and the Gospel: Christianity Justified in the Mind of Jesus,* appeared in the *British Weekly* of January 7, 1909.

is very good of you to do it yourself, and to make so much of it, and I assure you when you point out the places at which you differ from me I will give the most careful consideration to all you say.   It was a particular pleasure to me— to refer to a minor point—that in speaking of the style you could say ' no lingering.'   It is a good big answer to two questions, and I was not without apprehensions on this very matter.

The Church and the Kingdom don't clear up, somehow ; not that I have no ideas, but I have not seen or hit on a programme.   The Church is suffering in all Protestant countries at the present time from the persistent disparagement of it by preachers : we have run it down as if it had no real relation to living Christianity, and the lesson has been only too well learnt.   It is no part of the average Protestant creed any longer to say I believe the holy Catholic Church.   This, at least, is the theological aspect of the situation : no doubt there are many others.   In Germany the Roman Catholics, I believe, are gaining at the expense of the Protestants, and it is small consolation to say as Wernle does, that it gains those who were Romanists anyhow.   In this brilliant writer's last book—*Einführung in das theologische Studium*—there is incidentally a great deal of interesting light on religion in Germany.

What can become of a Church whose ministers

are trained by a man who writes that ' Jesus never made the slightest claim to sinlessness, much less to Godhead, and that as He is depicted in the oldest sources He would have positively shuddered at the idea that men should honour Him as they honour the Father.' In another place he writes, speaking of the displacement of Christianity in education, etc., ' Eine Menge *studierenden Theologen* sind aufgewachsen ohne die Anschauung christlicher Personen und ihres Glaubenslebens ; sie wissen tatsächlich nicht was christlicher Glaube ist.' Yet they have to keep the Church alive !

15 LILYBANK GARDENS, GLASGOW,
*January* 30, 1909.

Here is an article such as I have been able to do for next week.[1] As you will see from the last sentence, I can do one or two more, if you think this line is of any use ; I fancy the next one would have more flow in it. I hope your influenza has gone : you must have overdone yourself in Edinburgh. My sister-in-law heard you preach, and was much edified by the combination of skill and caution with which you manipulated your first pair of spectacles.

Let me thank you again most heartily for all

[1] ' Criticising the Church' (*British Weekly*, signed leader of February 4, 1909).

you have done for my book : I am sure your
articles will do good. About the conclusion, I
had some misgivings while writing it, in the
sense that I thought some people might read it
without reading anything that went before, and
those misgivings, by what comes occasionally to
my hearing, are to some extent being verified. I
am truly sorry for this, for I did not set out with
the conclusion in my mind, nor with any intention at all except to answer the two questions :
and apart from its relation to the premises I put
no importance on the conclusion. I am glad
that you like the body of the book upon reflection.
If it is not sound, then I have studied the New
Testament all my life in vain ; and in face of the
audacious and irresponsible writing about Jesus
which at present has such a circulation, I felt
bound to do what I could for what is to me the
foundation. I feel inclined to say when always
another and another book comes out by somebody
who can see everything in the Gospels but Jesus,
' From henceforth let no man trouble me ' : I have
*done* with this kind of cleverness. By the way,
where is Robertson Smith's article on the Place
of Theology, etc. ? I blush to say I have never
read it.

Your proposal about a Harmony does not
appeal to me. I always use one in my junior
class, and it is indispensable for a certain kind
of study, but there is no thoroughly satisfactory

I

way of making one, and there are plenty, such as they are. For some years I used Tischendorf's; these last two years I have used Huck's; and I have also worked, and got some of my class to do so, with Wright's. The English one, by Stevens and Burton, which Hodder and Stoughton published two or three years ago, is also very serviceable. Besides, before I print anything else I am going to work a lot more on the Epistles and rewrite all my lectures on Paul. I have given them for three sessions now, and found out what is the matter with them. I am going to Canada in April, but all the time I can command next summer I mean to spend on this.

15 LILYBANK GARDENS, GLASGOW,
*February* 6, 1909.

As I am not sure whether you have got away or not, I am sending this to Hampstead. It will do some other time if it is not wanted now. I hope you are in the sun somewhere. I read your letter with painful interest, especially your Monday in Edinburgh. When I was a minister one of the things I felt most constantly was the amount of sorrow there is of every description under apparently placid surfaces often; and I many a time regret that the kind of situation I now have tends to put this out of mind, and wish I had a congregation again—not that I have any morbid interest in pains or griefs, but just not to be so far away from what is too terribly real to so many.  Here, when I am not in College, I sometimes spend 24 hours without exchanging a word except with the girl who brings in my dinner, and as I am not one of the men who can work at reading or writing without end, the loneliness is long.

Our whole College affairs just now are in confusion.  With this £92,000 going to the Free Church, and the exhaustion of the Emergency Fund, I do not know what they will do.  Certainly they cannot give us another professor instead of Hislop, and when they fill up the vacancy in Edinburgh they must at once reduce the salaries all round.  I wonder that they have continued to pay us at the old figure all these years.  We have bought the College Church, and are taking it into the College in a way that will add greatly to our convenience and comfort, but will cost from beginning to end about £14,000.  Of this £7000 has been raised, and the financial board are appealing to friends of the College for the rest.  When it comes to the point, I fancy the Edinburgh vacancies will solve themselves.

I forgot to say that in your criticism of my book I felt the force of what you said about my not making more use of the ' mystical ' element in Paul's teaching—his consciousness of a present relation to Christ unparalleled by any relation to a human spirit living or departed : it was brought to my mind again by Mackintosh's article in *The Expositor*, which I liked. Apropos of your dissent from my remarks on the risen Saviour eating, I had a long letter from a lady of eighty, a life-long student of the Bible, as she told me. Since she was sixteen she had studied it daily, comparing Scripture with Scripture according to the excellent method taught her by the late Dr. Muir of St. Stephen's, Edinburgh. She entirely agrees with you, and argued the likeliness of our Lord's ' taking nourishment,' as she repeatedly called it ; but she wound up with a piece of the most audacious criticism I have ever seen.

In St. John 20$^{17}$ she says, ' I prefer (!) reading *Touch me* instead of Touch me *not*—as in Luke, *Handle me*, etc.' Isn't that good for eighty ? It shows how ' the wild living intellect of men ' will have its way. In this paper on the Church I have also kept off 'the body of Christ,' but I will bring it in later if you wish me to do more. There is no possibility of a book in them.

15 LILYBANK GARDENS, GLASGOW,
*February* 13, 1909.

I enclose another article on the Church [1] which I think you will agree with in the main.

[1] 'The Church and the Gospel,' leading article in the *British Weekly* of February 25, 1909.

I can do one or two more, but not next week.
It happens to be peculiarly occupied with
other things, but you will have Parliament
to keep you going.   I hope your influenza has
quite departed :   the weather here has been
intensely cold—colder than any time all winter.

Canon Hensley Henson sent me the other day
a copy of *The Churchman*, with an article in it
in which he refers to my book.   He agrees with
the things in it, apparently, with which you don't
agree, but he grieved me to the heart by describing me as an ' eminent Scotch Divine.'   It
sounded appallingly extinct in my ears, as if the
seal of oblivion had been set on my poor production almost before it had had time to see the
light.

15 Lilybank Gardens, Glasgow,
*March* 17, 1909.

It was extremely kind of you to wire to
me about the review in the *Times*, and also
to give it the publicity you did in the *B. W.*
(That is a compliment to the *Times* which I
did not intend when I began the sentence.)
It was friendly, and I presume will advertise the
book in another circle, but it did not strike me as
the work of one who had anything to overcome
in accepting the argument.   It seemed to me a
typically Anglican utterance—the traditional
Anglican, too, not the kind which will henceforth

be trained at Cambridge under Burkitt. Nevertheless I am glad it has been well spoken of even by a man who writes ' United Free ' in inverted commas.

I am sending with this a longish review of vol. v. of Ferrero's Rome.[1] When you sent me vol. iv., it was the first I had seen of the book, and I was extremely taken with it, so much so that I immediately bought all that had appeared of it in Italian. The consequence is that I have found it necessary to point out some provoking ways of the translator. Ferrero is an unusually picturesque writer, and abounds in comparisons which don't always suit English taste ; but this translator, by regularly leaving them out, quite takes the colour away from his author. The examples I have given are not the worst, and I could give literally dozens besides. Partly it is because they are morally or æsthetically disagreeable that he omits them ; but in nine cases out of ten it is just because they are difficult to translate. I presume there will be no more of it for a while, as the translator has overtaken the author and the author has gone to America to lecture for Roosevelt.

I hope the keen weather has not been bad for you. We had two days of west wind here which were heavenly, but most of the last fortnight has

[1] Vol. v. of Ferrero's book, *The Greatness and Decline of Rome*, was translated by the Rev. H. J. Chaytor, M.A.

been bitterly cold. I hope it may mitigate
before I sail on April 9.


15 LILYBANK GARDENS, GLASGOW,
*March* 30, 1909.

Many thanks for your letters. I read what
you said of Dods with the greatest interest
and sympathy, and share your feelings as you
look back on his constant friendship. He
was always the most generous of men. The
very first thing I wrote in the *B. W.* was a
review of his book on 1st Corinthians, and I
remember he wrote me from somewhere abroad
such a kind note about it. I don't wonder at
his decision about his MSS. Of course if the
editing had been left to you, it would have been
all right : but there is a great difference—at
least with me—between a MS. from which I can
lecture and preach, and one which I could send
to the printer : and we have had recent enough
examples of what can be done in the way of
injustice to the departed. I always have the
feeling, too, that in the kind of matter with which
he would deal, the public are not interested unless
the author is alive to stand by his opinion. On
Sunday I was in Edinburgh and heard of him :
so far as I could learn he seemed to be again in
a less critical condition.

Oddly enough, I had read last week both your

Gilfillan volume and Dr. Scott's book on the
Epistles. Thank you for the copy of Gilfillan.
I first read *Paradise Lost* in his series, and I
remember his introduction almost as well as the
solemn soaring sentence with which the poem
opens. What a full-blooded creature he must
have been. When I went to Broughty Ferry
I was introduced to his wife, and remember her
as a typical Scotch woman—massive head, plain
spoken, sagacious and kind. The ' new poets '
were a terrible lot, and it is difficult to keep from
laughing sometimes at Gilfillan's enthusiasm and
ideas of what is poetical and sometimes at his
paternal or avuncular criticisms of them.

On Macaulay and Burke he shows real insight,
though it seemed curious to me that he never
mentions any of Burke's finest work, and magni-
fies the *Letters on a Regicide Peace*, etc., which
could very well be forgotten. Your own introduction made me hope your History is under
way : it would be worth while dropping some
other things to secure it while so big a thing is
within your power. I hope to send another
article—perhaps two—before I go, which will be
some day next week.

15 LILYBANK GARDENS, GLASGOW,
*April* 8, 1909.

I go to Liverpool to-day and sail to-morrow
for Halifax. I am sorry that in the crowd of

other things I have not been able to do any more articles : but perhaps at Vancouver I may have more time for recollection.  At present I feel very distrustful of the organised action of the Churches to promote legislation even for Christian ends, or ends which can be represented as Christian, and perhaps if I said all I thought you might think it out of keeping with a journal of Christian and social progress. The multiplication of laws and the deterioration of character to a large extent keep pace with each other, and I believe it is one of the lessons the Church needs to learn that it can help society best by minding its own business, and letting the Legislature mind its.   There is a whole crowd of ministers going in for ' social ' reform, mainly because they have no Gospel; and because, like a certain class of politicians, they think this is the way to secure a following.  How to say this without throwing cold water on Christian zeal for improving the conditions in which people live, or without seeming to be heartless or in-different to the wrongs of the poor, may be difficult ; but it is just as needful to say Put not your trust in Parliament as Put not your trust in princes.  I am quite Johnsonian about all this kind of thing, and perhaps feel more like the eighteenth century than the twentieth.

I am sending Findlay's book on 1st John to David Smith, as I have not been able to do more than glance at it. It is every way an attractive book, but there is an excess almost of application and edification in it. Law's book has less of that, and, though some ministers will find less in it, most students will go through it with greater avidity.

I expect to be home by August 6, at the latest ; till then, any communication would reach me at Westminster Hall, Vancouver, B.C.

I hope you may have a good summer : it seems to have set in at last.

LAGGAN, ALBERTA,
*July* 18, 1909.

I have had a bad conscience about these articles on the Church ever since I left home, and now that I have got another off my mind, I am not sure that it is much relieved. But here it is anyhow. In Vancouver I was kept quite busy, between lecturing and preaching, but had on the whole a very good time. The Presbyterian Church there seems strong and active. The growth of the city is phenomenal, and the Church to a certain extent expands with it without an effort—a situation in which it is easy for men to become the victims of illusion. I was astonished at the size both of the churches and the congregations. The general methods of action, of course, affect church work also, and occasionally one was tempted to think that a church, in its determination to be practical and to deal with things as they are was giving itself to everything but the word of God and prayer. But the Church people, like all people here, are hopeful—and how much that means !

In British Columbia there is an immense amount of natural happiness due to the climate, the fertility of the soil, the certain but undefined chances of getting on, and so forth. The one thing about which people are really serious is the Japanese. They don't care a pin for the German Navy, and will never tax themselves a penny to build British dreadnoughts ; but the peaceful penetration of their country by the Orient makes them cold at the heart. The Japanese already monopolise the fisheries on the Fraser River, and are rapidly engrossing the labour, at least of the valuable timber trade, and they do not know how to resist them. While I was in Vancouver two Japanese cruisers visited the harbour, and it was curious to see the kind of courtesy the town extended to the officers—a mixture of deference and reluctance which could hardly have been mistaken by those to whom it was offered. The Canadians are intensely self-conscious about their nationality, and many of them have the absurdest ideas of their importance in the Empire, but they are deeply concerned about China and Japan. They know that they have no cruisers of their own, and the power of Japan on the Pacific is a menace from which they cannot escape for a moment. The unknown possibilities of it are the one thing, so far as I can see, which sober the imagination of this youthful race.

Although I have met with every sort of kindness here, Canada as a whole does not attract or exhilarate me, and I should not like to make it my home. I dare not say so aloud, but that is how I feel. I am no imperialist patriot, and one of the things in the *B. W.* I can never quite understand is its attitude to Rosebery ; but I love the poor Sparta I was born in better than the greatest of dominions, and I would rather be miserable in Glasgow than happy in Toronto or Vancouver. It cannot be news to you that the *British Weekly* is as readily and as regularly to be had in Vancouver as in Glasgow, and that a large number of Canadian and American ministers read it regularly. I knew this before, in a manner, but had not realised it, nor how very wide the circulation was. Armstrong sent me a lot of American reviews of my book, almost all of which quoted from your articles. Although I say it who should not, the quotations were almost the only intelligent things the reviews contained. I never saw such stuff. I do not say so because they were unfriendly ; on the contrary, they were meant to be commendatory and even laudatory in the extreme ; but three-fourths of them were written by people who had not the glimmering of an idea of what the book was about, and who evidently were total strangers to the situation to which it is addressed. If this represents the average intelligence of American Christianity it is ominous ; I am certain the poorest country newspaper in Scotland could command infinitely more competent hands for reviewing this kind of matter than seem to be at the disposal of the organs of considerable denominations in the States. Armstrong, however, was very well pleased with them from the publisher's point of view, and has reprinted the book, so that one ought to be grateful : if the buyers read it, they will get better value for their money—different value, anyhow, than the reviewers would lead them to expect. I have been staying here for a day or two, and go on to Toronto on Tuesday, where I have to preach on the 25th. On the 30th I sail from Quebec to Liverpool. I never was away alone for months before, and I do not think I will ever be again.

I hope you have had a good summer, and have a good holiday in view. Some time ago you wrote about the things people read, or did not read, in hotels ; there are about 300 people in this hotel just now, and no visible indications that they read anything. This is not yet a reading country. Books are dear and inaccessible ; ministers' libraries positively startling. I have seen several in which there was literally

nothing but dead matter. The intelligence of
the country is certainly mobilised, but it is
exclusively given up to commercial and practical
ends. They are alert to everything but man's
chief end. I have read none but old books, and,
though there is something valetudinarian in the
confession, I have not pined for new. One of
your correspondents lately mentioned that
George Meredith thought the xxivth Iliad the
finest poetry in the world, and having just read
through the *Iliad* again I assent with all my
heart. But why should a man who saw that
the finest poetry in the world was pure gold, as
it were transparent glass, have been content to
leave so much of his own poetry no better than
conundrums ? I felt never so much before the
dramatic as well as the epic value of Homer : the
truth with which Hecuba, Andromache, and
Helen are marked off against each other as they
mourn over Hector, is as wonderful as anything
in Shakespeare. This reminds me that another
book I have turned over is *Wilhelm Meister*.
But I cannot get on with it. The instinct for
reflection became a disease in Goethe. He culti-
vated it till he was bound to have *thoughts* about
everything and to write them down, whether the
Muse had inspired them or not, with the result
that he is responsible for a greater quantity of
sound platitudes than any great genius I know.
I am sure that to anybody but Schumann he must

often have been an insufferable bore. And as for all the profound reflections on the dramatic art in *Wilhelm Meister*, I had a thousand times rather study the Vincent Crummleses, and am only sorry I didn't put *Nicholas Nickleby* into my bag instead of *Meister*. But these are hardly Sunday thoughts, and I am going to preach to-night to as many of the guests here as will sacrifice their after-dinner nap to listen to the Gospel.

15 LILYBANK GARDENS, GLASGOW, W.,
*September* 30, 1909.

I was horrified the other day to lift the kind letter in which you welcomed me home, and to see that it was dated August 2. It did not seem so long ago, and I would have answered it sooner if I could have found it in my heart to write anything about Canada. But it would not have added to the happiness of anybody in Canada, not to say my own, if I had done so : though I had a happy enough time there and met with nothing but kindness.

What you said about Smith perturbed me very much : and we are still in suspense. On Sunday I was with Moffatt in my old church, and he reported on what was said to be the authority of Balfour of Burleigh that the offer of the Principalship had now been sent to Smith. If this is so, he will no doubt be lost to us. Though the

College and the city will both miss him more than I could tell, I think he ought to go. He has always been a loyal member of the United Free Church, and the place is one where such a man is needed and could do a great deal for the faith. But no possible successor could ever make up for him to me, and though I will be truly glad to see him put in so important a position I will be more unmitigatedly sorry to think of the College without him.

I saw you had some letters about the article on the Church and Legislation : the one by a Quaker, the second week after, struck me as particularly good. The others seemed rather to show how such an article is needed. I had quite a lot of letters about it too—more than about any casual thing I ever wrote. Most of them were evidently from evangelical old Tory gentlemen, who adore your religion AND abhor your politics, and I felt bound in common honesty to point out to some of them that what I wrote about was not the *B. W.* and Legislation, but the Church and Legislation, and that in point of fact I was on your side in politics as well as in religion, and only meant that while politics had a place of their own the Church was not that place. The most reasonable appreciative letter I had was from Dr. Robertson, the Moderator of the Established Assembly. He said he wrote because he knew I would be much attacked, and wished me to know that there were people who agreed.

I am sending four reviews with this : Bowne's *Studies in Christianity* [1] will be a seductive and impressive book to many, but he seems to me almost always just to stop short of what is most vital in the New Testament conception of Christianity. There is a lot of this kind of thing among Canadian Methodists, and I cannot be reconciled to it. I like lucidity as much as any one, but I like still better the sense of magnitude and even of immensity in a man dealing with revealed religion. Fog is abominable, but it is not so abominable as a man who thinks he has taken the measure of the breadth and length and depth and height, and that he knows all round what passes knowledge. The other books are hardly of any importance, and I was astonished to find two columns in the *Spectator* on Lady Mabel Lindsay's *Anni Domini*.

Carnegie Simpson spoke to me some time ago, in connection with a letter from you, about reviewing Rainy's life, and I said to him I would write an article on it if you asked me. But I was delighted to hear from him that you are going to do it yourself. It will not suffer from not being attacked enough. I do not know whether any one could have Boswellised Rainy; I only met him in private once, and his observations on

_____
[1] *Studies in Christianity*, by Borden Parker Bowne (Constable).

K

things were interesting : though one could not
speak of his ' copiousness of communication.'
Your article on Rosebery's Lichfield address was
interesting to me, and would have been even more
so if you had been severer on his want of appreciation for his subject.  The only thing in which
I don't agree with you (or with Johnson) is in the
appreciation of the *Ramblers*.   There is hardly
one of them, no doubt, in which there is not a
good sentence with the sap of experience in it,
but they are leaden and wooden on the whole.
The title of the Great Moralist was really earned
by the author of the *Lives of the Poets*, which are
a genuine criticism of life even more than of
literature ;  and win much of their interest in this
way.  I read the *Ramblers* as Rosebery says he
did *Rasselas*, but I will not read them any more,
whereas I hope to read in the *Lives* often.  Did I
tell you that a notice of my Johnson lecture in
Vancouver spelt his name with a *t*, and mine
without an *e* ?  Now could I write a column about
a country in which such things are possible ?

Do you think there is enough in the six articles
I have written to make even a very little book on
religion ?  I had an idea of writing another on
the Church and Education, but though we have
a great duty there which is not being done, and
for the neglect of which we are suffering under
new theologians and what not, the subject is so
complicated  practically,  that  I  don't  know

whether anything sufficiently definite could be said. It is getting to be quite an anxious question in foreign as well as home work, and is deeply exercising missionaries in China as well as in India and Japan. I hope you will keep well this winter to fight the battle of liberty : the taxes will be unpopular when they come to be paid, but the Budget is all right.

15 Lilybank Gardens, Glasgow, W.,<br>
November 12, 1909.

Allow me to say again, more deliberately, what a pleasure it was to see your name in the King's Birthday List. All your friends here rejoice in it, and if honours go by public service there must be few indeed whose title to them can compare with yours. *Stet fortuna domus*, as the pious Æneas says—unless my memory fails me. I hope you and all your house may long be happy in the enjoyment of this one.

We *are* terribly put out by the loss of Smith ; for some days I felt positively disabled by it. You can imagine what kind of colleague he is, and especially what he has been to me. We are of the same age, and though all four of us are on the friendliest terms, he and I were able to fraternise more completely with each other than with our seniors. He is not only the most genial of men, but what by no means always goes with geniality, the most truly unselfish; he always took with the utmost readiness not only his own share, but far more than his own share of the common work. I don't think I ever missed my wife more than the first few days after I knew he was going. I could not get away from it, and had nobody who could feel how much it meant. Nevertheless, I think he did right to go, as I told him beforehand, and though the far shining light of our College has departed we will hope for compensation elsewhere.

I had turned over the *Hibbert Journal* supplement before you sent it, and enclose an article on it. I never read such a production: the Plain of Shinar would have been a home of rest and a seat of light and leading in comparison with it. What struck me most in many of the papers was their conceit. It is like walking through a madhouse where everybody that talks talks about himself; and though there are *obiter dicta* of comparative sanity, the whole thing is as mad as Legion. R. J. Campbell, I think, is the very worst, and if something does not happen to him I should be really concerned about his future. Jones's article is really a review of the conclusion of my book: he wrote to me about it himself before it appeared. To me personally he is more than courteous, but I have put in a paragraph about him because he is far the most influential university teacher in Scotland, all our students are strongly impressed by him, and a good many who ought to be our students are diverted from the Church—and as I am convinced from the Gospel—by his influence. I swithered once whether I should do the article, partly because I was asked to contribute to the volume both by the editor and by Jones, who is one of the board, and partly because my name figures conspicuously in one of the really readable papers in it, but one may as well speak as think when he is in dead earnest.

15 LILYBANK GARDENS, GLASGOW, W.,
*December* 11, 1909.

The book of which I enclose a notice[1] is one of the best of the kind which I have seen for a long time. I do not know the author at all, except that he is a parish minister in Kirkcudbright somewhere : I have an impression that this is a kind of work in which more ministers are interested in the Established Church than in ours. I have been inclined to complain lately that we get plenty of philosophers but too few men who can parse ; but if we got the genuine article, like this, I should complain no more.

[1] *The Principles of Religious Development*, by George Galloway, M.A., D.Ph.

15 LILYBANK GARDENS, GLASGOW,
*January* 5, 1910.

Here are notices of the last two books you sent me. Ramsay and Miss Bell [1] are rather beyond me : I cannot form any estimate of the work of all these photographs for the history of architecture. But I cannot resist the impression that they have baked a huge cake with very little meal. As for Hawkins,[2] his book is the best of its kind, and I only wish for the sake of students it were half the present price.

You will be pleased to see how well the Central Fund has come out. No less than £38,000 was received in December, and there is more than enough to pay the dividend of £160 to each minister. Besides, we start fair for 1910, instead of with a debit balance of £9000, so that we ought to have an easy year compared with last. Everybody is grateful and encouraged, and all we want now is for those who were throwing stones at each other in a panic because they thought they were going to lose through each other's failure to do what was right by the Fund, to leave off recriminations and attend to the common good. There will be troubles within five years over town ministers who once depended in part on the Sustentation Fund, but who are now compelled

---

[1] *The Thousand and One Churches,* by Sir William Ramsay, D.C.L., and Gertrude Bell.

[2] *Horæ Synopticæ,* by the Rev. Sir John C. Hawkins, Bart.

to be self-supporting if they get any supplement, as they must, if they are to live at all; but sufficient unto the day is the evil thereof. Much may happen within the five years for which their personal interests are secured.

I have not written anything about the election, not because I am not on the Liberal side, but because I have no business to, nor anything particular to say. I hope to hear Churchill next Wednesday, whose address to the Dundee electors is the only thing of intellectual quality the election has yet produced.

15 LILYBANK GARDENS, GLASGOW,
*January* 29, 1910.

I have had a letter from one of our ministers, Mr. Muir of Rothesay, about a book he has written on the history of the relations of Christianity to Labour. He asks me to speak of it to you, as he would like to have it published by Hodder and Stoughton. I have not seen the book, which extends to about 85,000 words, he says: but I have known Muir since we were in College together—he was a year or two behind me—and think him an unusually able man. He was convener for a while of the Assembly's Temperance Committee, and had some legal experience before he became a minister; he is a B.L. as well as a B.D. There will not be anything unreal in his book, I am sure : he is a hard-headed man, and as a minister in a great variety of charges—Muthil, Glasgow, Blairgowrie, and Rothesay—he has seen all kinds of labour, and all kinds of relations between it and the Church. I know this will not make any difference to you or to Hodder and Stoughton, and that the book will be judged on its merits, but I should anticipate that its merits would be quite distinct.

I am glad to see you keep up your spirits about the election, and I am sure the Liberals who have been returned will be of the same mind. The only chance they have of life is to make no terms with the Tories. The mortification of the Tories over the Scotch elections is indescribable.

An interesting thing in that book of Montefiore's [1] is the proof it gives that the Church is full of Jews—people whose attitude to Jesus shows that they are at the O. T. not the N. T. stage of religion. The hundred and third Psalm is all they want, and they take it without misgivings, but the 8th chapter of Romans is only an embarrassment.

15 LILYBANK GARDENS, GLASGOW, W.,
*March* 28, 1910.

Here is a notice of Schweitzer's book, which I hardly thought would have been translated.

[1] *The Synoptic Gospels,* edited by C. G. Montefiore.

It is one of the most extraordinary books I ever read, but not nearly so important as the author thinks. Indeed the more I read in this line the more I feel the incomparable superiority of Strauss in sceptical power to any of his successors ; most of them live on crumbs that have fallen from his table. Both Sanday and Burkitt have made a great to do about his book, and as the translation is really masterly, it is certain to be much read. It is a curious phenomenon to see extreme scepticism about the history of Jesus driving men to appeal to St. Paul on the one side, and to the Catholic Church on the other, especially when the Catholic Church rejects the appeal as emphatically as I have no doubt St. Paul also would have done.

I am leaving to-morrow morning for Rome, and hope to be mostly there till the end of April ; by May 12 I must be back here. Perhaps you may get the general election over in my absence : it does not feel well for the Liberals at present. If Asquith is to be coerced by the Irish, and that in the interest of the whisky people who pay them, a great many earnest Liberals will not take the trouble to walk to the poll. The one moral of all that has happened is that there must not be any more equivocation in high places. I hope you may keep fit for the fight ; it is certain to give you work when you find out when it is.

15 LILYBANK GARDENS, GLASGOW, W.,
*May* 27, 1910.

I enclose a notice of Sanday's book,[1] which I found here when I came home. It was an evil hour for Sanday when he took Moberly and Du Bose for philosophers, and now that he has gone in for William James and Myers he is past praying for. I am sorry I cannot think his book likely to be of use, for he has been very polite to me in it.

I had a very good holiday in Italy, most of it in Rome. Pagan Rome impressed me much more than Christian—at least much more favourably. The pagans were not saints, but they were not habitually engaged in doing infamous things in holy names, and it gives them an honesty and dignity even in their badness to which most of the popes can make no pretence. I cannot understand how people who go to Rome can ever go over to the Romish Church. The whole thing rests so palpably on lies from top to bottom that it could have no effect on me but to make me a more determined Protestant than ever. I saw almost all the ministers in the Presbytery of Italy. A lot of them are wanting successors, ' young, vigorous men who will give their lives to the work,' but I must say I should hesitate to recommend any of these continental stations as his life work to a young and vigorous man. We

[1] *Christologies, Ancient and Modern,* by William Sanday, D.D.

want all our youth and vigour for more clamant needs.

I never spent six weeks from home during which so many of my own friends died.   There was some one every week—the last being Scott of Arbroath, the first man who asked me to preach for him when I was ordained in Broughty Ferry.   We had been friends ever since, and on the first Sunday of this year I preached for him.   He died just as my wife did, only more suddenly.

Yesterday afternoon I heard Rosebery speak of the King [1] at the University Council.   It was interesting because he knew him, but not otherwise remarkable.   The greatest charm about Rosebery's speaking is his voice : he has without apparent effort the right quantity and quality of it for any purpose.   I have never heard him eloquent, except in a literary sense—never in a flame of fire, as I once heard Gladstone denouncing the Cyprus Convention.   I hope you keep well and have your literary history in view. Do you expect me to read Frazer's book *through* before I review it ?   I sympathise with Johnson : ' One set of savages is very like another.'

15 LILYBANK GARDENS, GLASGOW, W.,
*May* 30, 1910.

I was out of town on Saturday, and did not get your telegram till it was too late to

[1] King Edward VII. died in May 1910.

answer till this morning. If I had not written such a long review of Sanday, I should have done an article on him, but I hope the enclosed may not be irrelevant. They will be giving in the Conference Reports at the Assembly as I write ; but I don't think it compromises the future of the proceedings for me to say what is here said.

15 LILYBANK GARDENS, GLASGOW, W.,
*June* 13, 1910.

You must not count on my writing anything about the Conference. I can only be there for part of two or three days, and my conscience smites me when I remember that some months ago I promised to speak at it. Whether it will interest the world outside I cannot tell : I have an impression that a great deal of what is called ' interest ' in the Church is artificial, and that when it comes to the point of doing anything it is exceedingly difficult to get it done. The Protestant Church has perhaps taught too exclusively the duty of consecrating to God the life we are born into, and left too little room for the truth that in this present evil world there must be great renunciations as well if there are to be great Christian careers. There is infinitely more talking about missions among young people than there used to be, much more knowledge too, and more of what are supposed to be ideas ; but though the student volunteer movement has fostered this, I question if it has increased by an atom the kind of enthusiasm which has the sense of duty in it, and which will materialise as self - denial. I hope I am not unkind to any one in saying this ; unhappily I think there is reason.

Your article on Vaughan [1] interested me very much, but though I appreciate his evangelical (?) poverty, I can't help saying of such men, Do not I hate them, O Lord, that hate Thee ? It is not evangelical poverty when a man buys even with all his money the power to enslave his fellow-men and to lord it over their faith. I had just as soon be Dives in the parable : the misrepresentation of Christianity and defamation of Jesus are not a whit worse or better in the one than in the other.

15 LILYBANK GARDENS, GLASGOW, W.,
*July* 1, 1910.

I am posting with this a long review of Bacon on John.[2] It is not an article, though it is as long as one, and perhaps it is not suitable to have a review out of proportion to others, though a shorter one would have to be too

[1] *The Life of Cardinal Vaughan,* by J. G. Snead-Cox.
[2] *The Fourth Gospel in Research and Debate,* by B. W. Bacon, D.D.

general. The book taken altogether is both brilliant and wrong-headed : it would be a fine book to go through, a chapter at a time, in a seminary : but the idea of offering it to the lay public to initiate it into the debate is astounding. The only conclusion to which the lay mind could come—and it would come to it promptly and decidedly—would be that, if ' John ' is anything like what Bacon thinks, the less we trouble ourselves about him the better. I would like to know whether Bacon really holds any conception of Christ's person which entitles Him to a place in Christian faith at all.

The criticisms of Scott in your letter this week were interesting. The *Fortunes of Nigel* was the first of the novels I read, and I quite sympathise with the readers in the Aberdeen library. I think it the best of those which are not the very best. Of all the opinions, the one I can least share is Barrie's on *Ivanhoe*. But for Rebecca, *Ivanhoe* is a story for boys ; at least that was my impression when I read it last. Though I belong to this quarter, and think Di Vernon and Bailie Nicol Jarvie both perfect, I am not sure that if I could only get one Waverley it would be *Rob Roy*. And for the *Fair Maid of Perth* I can get up no admiration at all. Was it not Dean Stanley who admired *Kenilworth* so highly ? I seem to have a lingering recollection of this sort. He had an enthusiasm for Scott altogether.

15 LILYBANK GARDENS, GLASGOW, W.,
*July* 16, 1910.

I had to write something about Frazer and get it off my mind, but I will send you an article next week. I hope you will get a good holiday at Lumsden : we have had summer here for some days such as I have not seen since I was a boy, but it is chillier again yesterday and to-day. Aberdeenshire is not a place for sunless weather. Some weeks ago I preached there, and had a motor ride in the afternoon on Saturday; the wind blowing through a thin cloth cap was as cold as ice on one's skull. But I need not talk to you about Aberdeen.

Dr. Ketler has made a hit in getting Ramsay, but I am not sure that Ramsay will be at home in Grove City. It is not the least like Oxford or Aberdeen. It will hold its aspiring head all the higher after being visited by so famous a man, but it is all on Ramsay's side already, so far as the New Testament is concerned, and therefore may not learn so much from him as from some one whom it might be tempted to contradict. I remember hearing him speak without MS. in the summer school at Aberdeen, and he was not very expert at it. But he was taking it very easily indeed.

I have no book in my mind at present, but am concerned about next winter's work at the hall. There are few indications of men giving them-

selves heartily to New Testament or other
studies, and I wish I knew how to excite a deeper
and more conscientious interest in them. We will
have David Smith giving his Bruce Lectures this
winter.

15 Lilybank Gardens, Glasgow, W.,<br>
July 21, 1910.

I enclose an article on the lines of the address
I gave to the ministers, and will do another,
but not (as at present disposed) on Self-
Sacrifice next week. At least not on that
alone. I have lately come across two interesting
criticisms of Protestantism by Catholics, out of
which I think I could do an article. One is by
Gratry, and is in short that Protestantism is
Christianity without sacrifice—no renunciations,
no mortifications, no good works. I could say
all I wanted under this head. The other is
by Brunetière, who makes it his charge against
Protestantism that it has ' intellectualised '
Christianity, and in doing so has robbed the
babes of their inheritance in it, and handed it
over to the wise and prudent. Between the two
there is enough to consider, perhaps to admit as
well as to answer, as will make an article. It is a
pity, for the purpose, that they are both dead.

I see you are very non-committal about
Woman's Suffrage. This is one of the things on

which I have a prejudice stronger than all reason, but quite convinced of its own rationality, and all the more so that philosophers like Balfour and Haldane take the lead on the other side. In spite of the majority for the second reading, I cannot think that most of the present electors have ever given it a serious thought, and when they do begin to think of it seriously I hope they will give their thoughtless representatives a piece of their minds—and the misguided women too.

15 LILYBANK GARDENS, GLASGOW, W.,
*July* 29, 1910.

I enclose another article. I had difficulty in getting a name for it, and if a better one occurs to you it will be a favour if you put it on. It is really on the subject you proposed ; it did not turn out feasible to combine it with Brunetière's criticism of Protestantism—or Calvinism, at least—for intellectualising Christianity. But both his remarks and Gratry's impressed me at the time.

15 LILYBANK GARDENS, GLASGOW, W.,
*October* 3, 1910.

I have written something on Eschatology in the Gospels, without much reference to von Dobschütz in particular.[1] His book strikes me as very good, conscientious and thorough, and

---

[1] *The Eschatology of the Gospels*, by Ernest von Dobschütz, D.D.

well balanced. Most of the recent books are
half-cracked. He has not been very fortunate
in his translator; there are a good many
blunders, evidently, though the sense can be
made out fairly enough.

I am going to London on Thursday, and must
leave again on Saturday, as I have to preach in
Birkenhead on Sunday. If you are in town I
hope to see you. The lecture I am giving to
Forsyth has to be published, but I don't know
whether they have any say in the matter. If not,
perhaps it would do for an article in *The
Expositor*.

What do you want done about the Expositor's
Greek Testament ? I don't like to say that only
the bits done by members of our Church—Dods,
Smith, and Moffatt—are well done, but that is
what I think. Moffatt's Revelation is by far the
best—he had the best chance ; but Dods' Hebrews
also seems to me about the most valuable thing
Dods has given us—exceedingly thorough and
interesting. Smith I like better than I anticipated, and I am sure ministers will find his
commentary very interesting.

15 LILYBANK GARDENS, GLASGOW, W.,
*October* 15, 1910.

Here is a notice of the Expositor's Greek
Testament, so long that if you think it is too

hard on anybody you can easily leave a bit out. I don't think it is, and have been as neutral about Hart and Oesterley as possible. Why it should be so difficult to get good expositors of Peter and James I don't know; but that they are still to seek is certain.

I hope you had a good holiday at Hindhead, and have come back fit for work. There was a capital attendance at my lecture, and when I have overhauled it a little I will send it up.

15 LILYBANK GARDENS, GLASGOW, W.,
*October* 22, 1910.

I enclose with this the lecture on Immortality [1] I gave for Forsyth. It is rather longer than I thought, and will contain about 9500 or possibly even 10,000 words. As it is much too long for an *Expositor* article, I suppose you will do what can be done to space it out into a little book.

Thanks for sending me the letter about Eschatology. I am going to write Mr. Carter this afternoon. I had a communication which touched me much more from a woman of seventy, a member of the Church of Scotland for fifty-four years, who holds Dr. Bonar's views about the Advent, and who was not so much puzzled as grieved. I would have written to her if I could, but the letter was anonymous, and gave no address.

[1] The Drew Lecture for 1910.

We have got a pretty good start at the College, I think; though we have more first year students of our own than we had last year, our total will not be quite so high. The number from abroad is smaller. I heard Haldane lecture to the New College Theological Society on Tuesday. He read the signs of the times in a Hegelian dialect of incredible abstractness which left most of his hearers in dumb bewilderment; if he had said what he thought in plain words, as he could easily have done if he had not been afraid to reveal his mind in that place, it would have caused not bewilderment but consternation. It was interesting, but not as impressive as I hoped.

15 Lilybank Gardens, Glasgow, W.,
*October* 28, 1910.

Many thanks for your letter. I am quite content that you should do as you think best about the lecture; it never occurred to me that such small beer would need to be ' travelled,' but I have no doubt you are right.

You did with the review of the Expositor's Greek Testament what I expected, and possibly what was best. It would not have helped any one to understand Peter or James to be told that Hart and Oesterley did not understand them—or at least that I thought so. I can understand afar off—if one may use Bible words in exactly the opposite of the Bible sense—your relief in seeing the last of it.   What you say of the Established Church people and the Conference interests me much because I cannot make them out at all, and have the feeling that the Conference members do not represent the Church at all.   The ordinary parish minister feels that his strength is to sit still, and that if he has only the sense to do so all the natural forces which determine the gravitation of human beings will tell in his favour, filling his church and emptying the rest.   Accordingly he is determined to sit still, and confident that if his position is affected in the slightest by any proposal of the Committee, he can dispose of the Committee without trouble.   Since College began I find it difficult to attend ;  it is impossible to give up one's class twice a month for the kind of discussions we have had.   Yet I am loth to lose contact with it.

15 LILYBANK GARDENS, GLASGOW, W.,
*November 5, 1910.*

I enclose brief notices of Forsyth [1] and Garvie.[2] I liked Forsyth more than ever, not because he was more lucid or consecutive, but because he really strikes sparks from his own anvil.

I was very much interested in your Chalmers, especially Part 2.   Did you happen to notice the

[1] *The Work of Christ,* by P. T. Forsyth, D.D.
[2] *The Christian Certainty,* by A. E. Garvie, D.D.

anti-union outbreak at last meeting of the Church of Scotland Presbytery in Dundee ?  Edinburgh and Glasgow overload the Conference, and though I hope this kind of ' Moderate ' malignity is not predominant, there is certainly a  great deal of it in the ordinary parish minister.  If one could judge by the Conference, the endowment difficulty might be settled easily enough, in view of the present difficulty we have in raising money for Church purposes :  people generally, whatever their abstract principles or preferences might be, feel that it would be silly to divert from such purposes £300,000 a year which comes in without doing anybody any harm.  But what the Church of Scotland people seem to find very hard to get into their minds is what is now an instinct in most of our people :  that they would not (as you put it for Chalmers) even ask the State to recognise Non-intrusion.  The two Churches seemed to have flowed since '43 in such entirely separate channels that their unconscious attitudes, on things like this, are for the moment unintelligible and incredible to each other.  But there will be some pronouncements by May.

15 LILYBANK GARDENS, GLASGOW, W.,
*December* 14, 1910.

I enclose one or two short notices of books I have had for a while : those that are in my line are not very important. I was sorry I could not think of anything for *The Expositor*, but between the College, the Church, and the City I am getting to be so hustled here that I can hardly think of anything at all. If anything comes in my way which I can make useful it will be a pleasure to send it ; but I have no distinct vision of a book—only a distant yearning towards one—from which chapters could be taken.

Some time ago I saw you speak of a Baskerville Greek Testament as a thing you might conceivably covet. I tried to get one for October 10, but failed : will you accept the one I am posting with this, and my belated congratulations and heartiest good wishes along with it ? I have often had an uncomfortable feeling that I was continually getting proofs of your friendship without indicating that there was anything corresponding on my side : of course I don't mean that this book puts that right, but only that it is a pleasure to me to think that it may give pleasure to you.

I saw Smith on Sunday night—looking very tired, I thought. Milligan was there also, who is evidently going to make a revolution in N. T. teaching at the University. It is a mercy to think that the O. T. and the New will both be effectively taught, whatever becomes of Dogmatic or Church History. What we want most among our students is still scholars. Philosophers used

to be our botheration, now it is economists, but
they have all souls above parsing,

15 LILYBANK GARDENS, GLASGOW, W.,<br>
December 23, 1910.

I don't much like reviewing my colleagues,
but I send with this a notice of Orr's work.[1]
It has all the materials requisite for making a
book and a good one, and he has also all the
requisite powers : but there is something that
' crowds and hurries and precipitates ' his utterance without making it in the least like the
nightingale's song. It is rather like the extempore speech of a well-equipped Parliamentary
candidate who interrupts every sentence to
give a slap—often an effective and resounding
one—to some audacious person who has inter-
rupted *him*. But I wish he had taken a little
longer, and left a more comfortable impression
of having an easy rather than an excited mastery
of the situation.

I have just read Dods's letters, and agree with
you heartily in your admiration of the man.
What struck me most in them were the few
sentences about Rainy. Dods had evidently
read him accurately from the first, and his character was not appreciably modified to the last.
His pride, his ' profanity '—by which I suppose

----

[1] *Sin as a Problem of To-day*, by James Orr, D.D.

he means that he was at bottom a humanist and in no internal bondage to any *form* of Christian religion—his scientific quality of intelligence, all the things, in short, which impressed me in him when he was old, were evidently conspicuous from the first.   I am not sure that I should rate the letters generally as high as you do.   For one thing, they seem to me to have a certain scarcity of ideas.   In preaching, Dods had in a higher degree than any man I ever knew the power which is most to be coveted by a preacher—that of making the obvious impressive ;  but though this is invaluable in ' practical ' literature, if one may use such an expression, it is hardly enough for a book which you read not to do you good, but to give you pleasure.   The position of a probationer, too, without a call, is hardly wide enough in its appeal to furnish the basis for a classic.   I was astonished to learn what I might have known that Dods was ordained at thirty. Why, I was thirty myself when I was ordained, and so are plenty of respectable men whose names never pass into proverbs.   But to many in this generation the book will be extraordinarily interesting, and I hope it may be a great success.

15 LILYBANK GARDENS, GLASGOW, W.,<br>*January* 16, 1911.

I am much obliged to you for writing about Dr. Dixon's *Study of the Criminal,* and have told him to send it direct to the publishers. I want to ask your advice now on my own account. Some time ago I had an idea of printing my little book, *The Atonement and the Modern Mind*, ALONG WITH *The Death of Christ.* The former is now out of print, of the latter there are only about 200 on hand; and Mr. Stoughton has written to me about the idea of printing the two as one volume—*The Atonement and the Modern Mind* being simply appended as a supplement to the other book. It could be published at 7s. 6d., with a page like that of *Jesus and the Gospel,* only not so widely spaced. What do you think of this? I am anxious that people should read *The Death of Christ,* but while I think some would take to it the more readily because of the appendix, I know that many men will buy a 6s. book who draw the line at a 7s. 6d. one. I have the same kind of prejudice against the combination as I would have against anything which pretended to be new, and was not really so, and I think I can say sincerely that I am quite indifferent as to how it turns out financially; but if you could give me your mind on the idea in general of printing the two books as one, I should be much your debtor.

I will think about the Expositor's Bible Class Text Books, and write again.

15 LILYBANK GARDENS, GLASGOW, W.,
*January* 21, 1911.

It was very good of you to give me the
benefit of your judgment so promptly, and it
has quite disposed of the difficulty I had about
Mr. Stoughton's plan. I did not like the idea
of offering in a new shape what was not sub-
stantially new; but I will be delighted to revise
the whole—which will not imply any material
change—and to make the new book 6s. is exactly
what I should have wished. About the Expositor's Bible Class Text Books I am not so
clear, except on the one point that I must not
undertake one. I have always thought that
the little volumes of Dr. Maclaren were just
about the *ne plus ultra* in this kind, and I don't
know how any one could improve on them. It
is certainly a drawback to most recent commentaries that the study of criticism has apparently blinded the commentators to the fact that
the books on which they are working are bits
of the Bible—that but for that fact they would
in all probability never have reached us—and
that the chief business of the commentator is
to elucidate their significance as vehicles of
revelation : nevertheless, I don't see very well
how a simple set of books, covering the whole
Bible, could be written with this in view. The
helps that are published annually for S. S.

Teachers, and that will continue to be published, must always be the first resort of those who actually want this kind of help. For myself, I feel that, if I am to get doing what I want to do, I must not undertake any odd jobs like this. The notes in the *Homiletic Review* were not exacting, for the subjects were those on which I am lecturing all the time, and the space to fill was small. But I really want some day to write something about St. Paul and his Gospel, and if I don't let it accumulate in my mind I will not get on at all.

I am sorrier than I can tell about Simpson [1] leaving us. I have seen a great deal of him, and he has been growing every year in weight both of mind and character. There is no one on our side in these Conferences with the Church of Scotland who can state our case as incisively and impressively as he, and we are bound to miss him dreadfully. We have been very intimate, for many reasons, and I will miss him more than anybody in the Presbytery. I do hope when he goes that he will be able to concentrate his mind on preaching, and make a spiritual impression on his new place. He really knows what religion is, and is capable of being a good stronghold for it in an indifferent place.

[1] The Rev. P. Carnegie Simpson, D.D., now Professor at Westminster College, Cambridge.

15 LILYBANK GARDENS, GLASGOW, W.,
*February* 3, 1911.

I am sending with this the article on Hobhouse.[1] He is too good for his company, and if he only keeps on will make a very good Free Churchman some day.

It is out of the question for me to do a book on Matthew. It is literally the most difficult thing in the world to do, and if I ever tried it I should like it to be the best thing I ever did, not an impromptu effort, as anything I could attempt just now would be. The sermons don't seem so incredible, and I have sometimes thought I had a good title for a volume—Sermons on Texts. I am very much dependent on my text, as a rule, and have spent much pains in trying to get students to treat their texts with proper respect, and to give them an innings in their sermons somewhere.

This is our fourth continuous day of dense fog, and I am thankful to think of getting out of it to-morrow : I am going to spend the week end with Smith. I hope you may have sunshine in the Riviera : here we cannot see from one street lamp to the next.

---

[1] *The Church and the World in Idea and in History*, by Walter Hobhouse, M.A., Canon of Birmingham Cathedral. (Leader of February 16, 1911.)

15 LILYBANK GARDENS, GLASGOW, W.,
*March* 15, 1911.

I did not send my Murtle Lecture because it was not appropriate for *The Expositor*. It was too much of a sermon, and though it could be carried off by energetic delivery, I could have taken no pleasure in seeing it printed. I am sending with this a notice of the Oxford *Studies on the Synoptic Problem*,[1] a really valuable and interesting book, at least to students. The one thing I feel sure of in the whole business is that the ' documentary ' idea of sermons has been driven far too hard and exclusively, and that there must be a far ampler recognition of the fact that the Gospel matter was widely known, and also freely reproduced, apart from documents, even by people like Luke and Matthew, who certainly had documents at command. Oral tradition alone cannot explain some of the phenomena, but there are some which can be naturally explained by nothing else.

15 LILYBANK GARDENS, GLASGOW, W.,
*April* 15, 1911.

I enclose two notices of books, and one of the Ancient Literature ' sample ' of the *Encyclopædia Britannica*. The *Encyclopædia* is a wonderful book,

---

[1] *Studies on the Synoptic Problem*, by Members of the University of Oxford, edited by W. Sanday, D.D.

and it is also being wonderfully advertised, but it beats me to express any opinion about Babylonian, Celtic, and Syriac literature. Monro's article on Homer is worth any money, but it is the only article in this sample for which I would have given money. I was very much taken with Macfadyen's book,[1] and think it one of the most unfeignedly and earnestly religious books I have read for long. The only thing I don't quite like in it is a leaning he has to the psychical research and subliminal consciousness people : but he has enough of critical faculty to keep them from doing him much harm.

I am to be in Broughty Ferry next Sunday for Moffatt, and in the week after am preaching for the Baptist Missionary Society at Bloomsbury. I expect to be two days with Forsyth, and will hope to see you if you are at home.

15 LILYBANK GARDENS, GLASGOW, W., *April* 21, 1911.

The reason why I cannot give you the Murtle Lecture for *The Expositor* is not that there were suffragettes in it—no such thing : I was rather proud of the bit about St. Paul and women—but that the main part of it was about Propitiation, and that I have used up in the sermon I am

---

[1] *Truth in Religion: Studies in the Nature of Christian Certainty,* by Dugald Macfadyen, M.A.

going to preach to the Baptists about Missions. But when I come back I will try to think of something else.

Many thanks for arranging about the lecture on Immortality. I have just revised and sent it back to Messrs. Hodder and Stoughton. To-night I preach for Moffatt, and on Sunday dispense the Communion in my old church. It is exactly twenty-five years since I did so the first time.

15 LILYBANK GARDENS, GLASGOW, W.,
*May 5*, 1911.

I enclose a notice of Moffatt which I think does him justice, and should be understanded of all who take interest in these things. I have just glanced at the book on Miracles,[1] and will write something on it if I can ; but except that the man does not believe in miracles at all I don't see very much in it. Your leaders on the Church are very much to the point; everything is down in our Presbytery just now—membership, Bible Classes, Sunday Schools, all kinds of societies.

Though it is my business to teach, the one thing I covet is to be able to do the work of an evangelist, and that at all events is the work that needs to be done.

[1] *Miracles in the New Testament*, by the Rev. J. M. Thompson.

15 LILYBANK GARDENS, GLASGOW, W.,
*May* 13, 1911.

After thinking over this book of Thompson's
I thought better of it, and enclose some reflections upon it. I might have headed it Rationalism in the Church of England, but it is not
exactly what ought to be called rationalism,
and the author's use of words which sound
orthodoxly, but cannot be meant so, is of quite
another school. Except for his position, it
is not really a book of any importance. His
critical knowledge is slender, and he depends
with no attempt at verification on wild men like
Bacon. But the people who don't believe in any
miracles don't disbelieve for the kind of reasons
alleged here, so that it is of less account if these
are inaccurately given. What struck me most
in the book was to find a man writing a volume
about Christianity in which no account was
anywhere taken either of sin or salvation.

15 LILYBANK GARDENS, GLASGOW, W.,
*June* 13, 1911.

One of our ministers, Reyburn of Kirkintilloch,
has written a book on Calvin, which he wishes
to publish, and asks me to speak of it to
you. He has shown me some chapters, and it
seems to me to be done with great thoroughness, and on a sufficiently ample scale. Shall

M

I ask him to send it to you, or direct to Messrs. Hodder and Stoughton? He has it all typewritten, so that it is easily read.

We are having a summer school here this week, and had lectures this morning from Oman, Milligan, and Cairns. To me, Oman's was much the most interesting; he has something very original and penetrating in his mind when he deals with the philosophical side of theology. In Milligan's lecture on papyri there could not be anything new, and Cairns on the reflex influence of missions on theology was attractive rather than stimulating. Our new hall did not seem to suit him very well for speaking in : it holds about 400, and as there would be only 100 or so present, there was a large surface of wood exposed—a bad condition acoustically. I am going to give two lectures on Criticism and the Parables—one on the transmission, and one on the interpretation of parables—at the end of the week ; if you like, I will send them for *The Expositor*.

*The Golden Bough* has nearly killed me, and though it is impossible not to admire Frazer's learning and industry, it is impossible also not to feel what unattractive things learning and industry may be. He says he has never studied Hegel, and gives some extracts supplied by a friend ; but I could have reminded him for his good of an *obiter dictum* of Hegel that ' learning is the knowledge of things which have no value

except that others don't know them.' I hope
the endless summer suits you, and that you will
enjoy even the Coronation.

15 LILYBANK GARDENS, GLASGOW, W.,
*June* 27, 1911.

Here are the two papers on the Parables
—one on their transmission, the other on
their interpretation—for *The Expositor*, and
two reviews for the *B. W.* Carpenter's book [1]
leaves a curious impression on one's mind as
of a man asking every kind of question
about Jesus except the question which Jesus
asks. Like Wernle in his review of my book, he
seems to think it possible to be a thoroughly
good Christian and yet flatly refuse to take
Jesus at His own estimation. I confess this
is too remote from any comprehension of the
whole matter I can compass for me to argue very
directly with it. You may call Jesus Lord, and
be a Christian ; or refuse to do so, and not be a
Christian ; but it is absurd to think yourself a
Christian when your attitude to Jesus is that of
vigilant jealousy that He shall not invade your
freedom, nor come between you and God—
tempered with an admiration not free from patronage. This is what the philosophy of religion
brings some men to.

[1] *The Historical Jesus and the Theological Christ,* by J. Estlin
Carpenter, D.D.

15 Lilybank Gardens, Glasgow, W.,
*July* 8, 1911.

Many thanks for Mrs. Gibson's books. I only know enough of Syriac to spell out various readings, and would not dream of exposing myself in this region in *The Expositor* ; but when I read the translation I will perhaps be moved to write a few lines which could serve to advertise it, and you could do with them as you liked. I read your notes on Rosebery with much appreciation. I have no hesitation in agreeing with him on two main points—that *Vanity Fair* is incomparably Thackeray's greatest book, and that *Esmond* is odious. In the last point I can appeal to my wife's opinion as even more decided than my own. As for the greatest novel in the language I should not like to give an opinion. I have only read *Clarissa* and *Tom Jones* once, and it is now a good while ago : but as I have not felt compelled to read either of them at least three times, I have that reason to start with for preferring *Vanity Fair*. The most widely read novel reader in my acquaintance, and a very able person to boot, pronounces unhesitatingly for *David Copperfield*. My sister-in-law votes Laura a bore, and I confess, in spite of her virtues, I have sometimes thought she could be adduced as evidence that Lamb was right when he said that *any* woman could marry *any* man if she just made up her mind to—or something to that effect. About George Eliot I sometimes agree with Dr. Maclaren and sometimes with Lord Acton : she is only good—and then no one can be better—when she is dramatic ; when she is herself, she is like other preachers out of pulpits.

Old Dr. Carslaw wants you to publish some kind of book of prayers for him, and I am telling him just to send it to Messrs. Hodder and Stoughton. The prayers are not his own, but borrowed from various sources from Augustine to Walsham How, and the book would have about 19,000 words.

How many sermons are wanted for a volume ? Mine, I should think, average about 4000 words— an odd one, perhaps, 4500. There would be no objection, I suppose, to putting in one or two the substance of which has appeared at some time or other in the *B. W.* ? I find it irksome to write them as I rarely read.

15 LILYBANK GARDENS, GLASGOW, W.,<br>July 31, 1911.

I enclose two reviews—one of a very live, and the other of a very stodgy book. I never came across anything of Osborn Taylor's before, but it is first rate.[1] Plummer, on the other hand, is

---

[1] *A History of the Development of Thought and Emotion in the Middle Ages*, by Henry Osborn Taylor.

stolid to the last degree : his book might have been written fifty years ago, and is not as good as Evans, Edwards, Findlay, or any of the standard books we have.

Don't you think Ramsay on Moffatt has been very scrappy and unedifying ? I don't see what on earth Moffatt has to reply to. He has not taken a single historical problem in the book and shown in detail where and how Moffatt has gone wrong ; and as for his talking down to him and lecturing him, while a Christian might be tempted to retaliate, I suppose it is a temptation to be overcome.

The heat here is still oppressive, and I suppose worse with you.

15 LILYBANK GARDENS, GLASGOW, W.,
*August* 19, 1911.

I was glad to hear, what you thought about Ramsay on Moffatt, and though I agree with a great deal of it, I still think Ramsay made very little of his three papers. I shall be astonished if Moffatt answers, not because he will think them unanswerable, but because there is nothing specific in them which calls for a reply. Gregory in his recent pamphlet says there are not more than five men in the world who could undertake to produce a critical text of the N. T. ; as he does not name them, I don't know whether he includes Souter ;

Souter's own edition is certainly an exceedingly valuable and useful book. The one thing I do regret in the method of Moffatt's book is the way in which it is overladen with opinions which are of no consequence in the world, and the one thing for which I value it is, that at every point, whether you agree with him or not, it suggests questions to the mind. It is not that everything is in flux, though for him this is perhaps too much the case, but that you become aware that there is something further to be investigated and to be learned on every point. I agree that as it stands his books will not have the authority or the permanence of Driver's, but I should never think of comparing him to a wild man on a monoplane like Bacon.

I sent an article on St. Paul and Women, but I suppose the labour insurrection makes every subject but one untimely. Mrs. Pankhurst was at Largs last night arguing that the unrest shows how necessary it is to have women taking part in domestic legislation. Most people, I should think, if they drew any inference from public affairs at this moment, would draw them in the opposite direction. However, my innocent article has nothing to do with ' thae unfidel suffragettes,' as Sara Handy calls them.

It gave me a little shock to see my sermons advertised as Sermons on Texts—a title which amused me a little as at once despairing and pro-

vocative, but which was no fixture in my mind.
I have since had a notion to call them Bible
Commonplace, or The Ministry of the Word, or
something of that kind. What I meant to
suggest by the name was that they were sermons
in which the text did the preaching, and that
the one claim made for them was that they were
Biblical; but I suppose I can call them anything
yet in spite of the advertisement. They will be
finished, anyhow, by the end of next week, and
I will get away for a holiday at last. We have
been in Glasgow all summer, and the heat has
been very trying.

15 LILYBANK GARDENS, GLASGOW, W.,
*September* 29, 1911.

I have just found the books to-night on re-
turning from Grantown, and will let you know
what I think of them in a day or two. I infer
from what you say that you don't want an
article on Wendland unless it can be cordially
appreciative.

Probably you know that Dr. Patrick of Winni-
peg has died. He and I have been friends for
thirty years, and I should like to send a short
notice of him to the *British Weekly*. He was
well known in our Church, but owing to superficial peculiarities never valued as he should have
been. A more absolutely unselfish man never

breathed. I will post what I write on Sunday, which will, I presume, be in good time.

I had a month in Grantown, and enjoyed it exceedingly. What you said in one of your letters about the keenness of the air where there are no trees struck me in that region. I walked one day with my sister-in-law from Tomintoul to Grantown, and had the same sort of atmosphere as you delight in (or boast of) on Donside. I hope you are back fit for the winter.

15 LILYBANK GARDENS, GLASGOW, W.,
*November* 16, 1911.

I enclose a few more reviews. I liked Forsyth's book [1] very much. It is wonderfully free from his usual peculiarities ; and though a great deal of it is written in a region in which I am in no wise at home, it seems really full of ideas and interest. Its tendency to great generalisations is not congenial to me ; in fact I cannot help being sceptical about them ; and there is a fair proportion of things which you cannot say are untrue, but are probably just as true as the opposite. On p. 264 he ventures into Greek, and uses σύγγνσις as in contrast to σύνθεσις in a sense which is quite impossible. That reminds me that I had a letter from Margoliouth standing up for his ' greaves of

---

[1] *Christ on Parnassus : Lectures on Art, Ethic and Theology*, by P. T. Forsyth, D.D.

new wrought tin,' with an undertone as of one suggesting that he did not expect to be understood by or convince everybody : which I acknowledged as well as I could.

15 LILYBANK GARDENS, GLASGOW, W.,
*November 25, 1911.*

As you will see, I have written a long notice of Lake.[1] It is a really important book, and in some essential points I think a thoroughly misleading and pernicious one. I don't care a straw whether the Galatians were ' north ' or ' south,' and the present adherence to Ramsay is to a large extent as much a matter of fashion as the size of ladies' hats ; but this reduction of Christianity to one of many ' redemptive ' religions which struggled for victory and survival in the early centuries, the most religious period our race has ever known, and the identification of the Christian sacraments with pagan mysteries, which is partly the alleged basis of this, and partly an inference from it, is serious, and I have taken space to be explicit about it.

I am sorry you are going in for the woman's vote in politics. Manhood suffrage, on the basis of universal military training—a vote to every

---

[1] *The Earlier Epistles of St. Paul: their Motive and Origin*, by Kirsopp Lake.

person of twenty-five who had put in his drills—
is the panacea which commends itself to me.   If
we had any more demonstrations like Mrs. P.'s
last, I should say, ' Do not hesitate to shoot ! '
I admit this is a subject on which I can get few
to agree with me, and that my dear wife was, as
her sister is, altogether on the wrong side.


15 LILYBANK GARDENS, GLASGOW, W.,
*December* 8, 1911.

You have always been much more than generous to any writing of mine, but the way in
which you speak of my sermons [1] quite over-
whelms me.   You must believe I am grateful,
and not for this only, though I do not know
how to do more than flatly say so.   Though
I gave up the idea of calling them ' Sermons on
Texts,' I am glad you noticed that they are
textual ;   I don't know how a minister gets on
at all who does not let the text preach.   There
was one thing in your notice of Maclaren which
gave me a thrill of joy—the sentence about his
boots.   Many and many a time when I have been
baffled by a sermon—or by something else—in the
forenoon, I have found no way out but to get up,
put off my slippers and put on my boots and a
coat, collar and tie in which I could go out ;   it
usually had the effect of bringing my desultory

[1] *The Way Everlasting,* Sermons by James Denney, D.D.

faculties to the scratch. But I had no idea I was in such distinguished company, though I remember Scott used to take an hour in the morning to shave, dress, and put on his shoes, having an energetic contempt for the dressing-gown and slippers mode of life. Most people, in spite of these high examples, will have a sneaking sympathy with Descartes, who created the higher mathematics while sipping brown soup under the blankets in broad day.

Welch, who has been delivering the Kerr Lectures in our hall on the religion of Israel under the kingdom—the religion of the Genesis stories, of Elijah, Amos, Hosea, and Isaiah—asked me to introduce them to Hodder and Stoughton with a view to getting them published. Perhaps you will pass this on to them and let it count as an introduction. I think them unusually good lectures, perhaps with some crankiness, but really powerful and stimulating, and very well adapted to revive interest in the Old Testament, which seems for a time to have flagged among us. 'Under the Kingdom' does not include Jeremiah, but does include Deuteronomy : he could not bring Jeremiah in within the limits he set himself.

I see in the papers to-day the death of Charles Thomson, who took the Hebrew Class here during Smith's first year in Aberdeen : a most promising life cut short.

Warm congratulations on the semi-jubilee of the *B. W.* It is the semi-jubilee of my ordination.

15 LILYBANK GARDENS, GLASGOW, W.,
*December* 16, 1911.

I have read with much interest your article on Immortality,[1] and I think I agree with it all. To say Christ would not have done and suffered what He did for beings less than immortal is probably the simplest and truest way to bring His work into relation to the question of immortality, but it assumes a certain view of what He did and suffered. I should never dream of being dogmatic about conditional immortality; it seems to me to have all the marks of a half-way house about it, and I cannot think it will ever be more than a flitting and vanishing idea in this region. But from the point of view taken by Dale, is it not arguable that Christ might have done and suffered all He did do and suffer for people who had the capacity of immortality, but had forfeited it by sin, yet were capable through Him of being restored to it again? If we speak of Jesus as acting on motives, is not the motive of putting immortality within the reach of mortal men, or blessed immortality within the reach of lost men, one

---

[1] 'Immortality in the Light of the Cross.' (Leading article in the *British Weekly* of December 14, 1911.)

on which we can interpret His life and death ?
What I feel is that it is unreal to separate life
and blessedness, or death and doom, and that
you seem to say that unless man was bound to
have for ever a being which is not determined
either way Christ's work is unintelligible. I don't
like to forbid a man to preach Christ who only
feels able to say that to men whose future apart
from Christ is ' all unknown.' Christ came to
bring, at the cost of His cross and passion, life
and immortality. But as I can hardly think you
would forbid this either, it is possible I may not
have exactly seized your mind. The sermon on
immortality is one I must have written about
twenty years ago, and I never preached it but
once since. It does not preach well, but I thought
the substance of it would be instructive to some
when read, and accordingly I put it in. When I
left Broughty Ferry I burned nearly all my
sermons, and was horrified as I did so to see what
an amount of repetition there was in them ; I
have the same horror, only worse, when I look
over them in print.

15 Lilybank Gardens, Glasgow, W.,
*December* 23, 1911.

I enclose with this a review of Ward's book.[1]  It

[1] *The Realm of Ends; or, Pluralism and Theism.*   Gifford Lectures,
by James Ward, Sc.D.

is extraordinarily interesting for this kind of thing, and keeps closer to reality than metaphysicians usually do. But he has a curious way when he encounters a difficulty, of saying, ' But first we must '—raise some other very remote question, which is apt to put out a reader who finds it difficult enough to hold a single thread in such abstract discussion. On the whole, however, it is decidedly on the Christian side, and therefore a book to be thankful for. I meant to have sent with this a notice of De Witt Hyde's book on *The Five Great Philosophies of Life*,[1] but I left it lying in a shop in Edinburgh on Tuesday, and, though I sent stamps at once to return it, there is no sign of it yet. I had read about two-thirds of it, and thought it excellent, a really happy specimen of modernising and applying the ancients without traducing them at all.

I hope you are going to have a rest at Christmas ; we are going to Crieff on Tuesday for a week : our holidays, you will have a malicious joy in hearing, are longer than usual. Like you, I have sometimes wondered at Dickens's representation of nonconformity in people like Stiggins, but I think I understand it apart from any personal reason. All the novelists like Dickens, Thackeray, and Fielding represent the *natural man* and his goodness—that is, goodness

---

[1] *The Five Great Philosophies of Life*, by William De Witt Hyde, President of Bowdoin College.

in *instinctive* forms; but all sorts of nonconformity stand for goodness in *reflective* forms—that is, in forms which have a tendency to be self-conscious, and, if they are not watched, Pharisaic. Now self-consciousness and Pharisaism are very odious to the natural man, whose goodness must be impulsive and instinctive or null, and hence he pitches into them whenever he gets the chance, with or without provocation.

I was struck once by a remark of Birrell in his life of F. Lockwood, to this effect: that Lockwood had not a particle of a nonconformist about him; he was born in the Church of England and on the edge of Doncaster Racecourse, and saw no reason why a man should not be equally at home in both. That is the sort of man Dickens understands, but a man who takes away these congenial environments and gives nothing as good in their place, he delights to represent as an odious humbug. I think I sympathise with this quite enough to understand it, and even to see a certain justification for it; but the novelists should have had good nonconformists as well as bad. I believe they would have had but for the feeling that goodness must be spontaneous and not a matter of ' principle ' at all. A character that implies dissent implies comparison, and comparison is odious.

15 LILYBANK GARDENS, GLASGOW, W.,
*January 24, 1912.*

It was very good of you to write me so long and interesting a letter at Christmas. Immortality is a vast subject, and in a sense identical with Christianity ; the Gospel cannot be described at all unless it is described as a victory over death as well as sin. At least this is always how the N. T. describes it, but I admit the great mass of people even in our Churches agree on this point rather with Mrs. Moncure Conway than with the Apostles. But though this is natural, it is not spiritual ; the inner man ought not to be exhausted with the outer, but to be renewed day by day. In what I said about reunion I rather reported what seemed to me the historical fact than indicated what should be. I was astonished to find so little evidence in anything I had read that the desire for reunion tended to produce faith in immortality. Where such faith has originated, of course, it is brought to bear in this direction, but I found no proof to speak of that the desire for reunion originated faith. But I may be quite mistaken as to the fact from not having read in the right direction.

I suppose you will have had a little book called *In Dickens Street* sent you for review. I wish you could do it yourself. The writer, W. R. Thomson, is one of our ministers whom I know very well. He is also one of the ablest men I

N

have ever met, and I think this series of sketches shows a quite extraordinary appreciation of Dickens—a genius in fact for appreciation not unworthy of Dickens' genius for creation. Although they appear at the Centenary time there is nothing *ad hoc* or *pro re nata* about them ; they are thoroughly mature. Thomson, who used to be in Caledonia Road Church here, went out to South Africa for five years for the sake of his boy's health, and is now settled in a little church at Bellshill. But his shoulders are broad enough to bear any burden.

I enclose reviews of two philosophical books. Freeland Barbour's book pleased me very much.[1] It is a book of a sort that is really wanted, and it would do good if it were read in Universities. The other, the American book which I lost and recovered, is also excellent in its way. It is full of animal spirits as well as of intellectual vigour ; the man's mental digestion is so good that he can assimilate all kinds of nutriment and dispose with buoyancy of Epicureans or Stoics or Platonists or what you please. There is a noble Christian assurance about the whole thing too which it does one good to meet ; only it is too dear at 6s. 6d. net.—too dear, I mean, for the size.

I hope you have had a holiday and are feeling fit for the spring. Evidently it is going to be turbulent, and the mere fact that so many people

[1] *A Philosophical Study of Christian Ethics*, by G. F. Barbour, D.Ph.

are thinking about the future of the Government is a more convincing proof that its future is risky than any arguments to the contrary will outweigh. But good luck to them—except in their Women's Votes business.

15 LILYBANK GARDENS, GLASGOW, W.,
*March* 11, 1912.

I enclose a few more reviews. One of the books—Humphries on the Holy Spirit [1]—is very good indeed. The London Theological Faculty have not made a very auspicious start, and their volume [2] will not bear comparison with the Cambridge Biblical Studies. It does contain some excellent papers, but some also very poor. But what does it matter as long as the strike lasts? Does any one buy books or read them just now? With your last leader I sympathised rather than entirely agreed. Something seems to have gone to the heads of the massed masses that persuades them they have only to say they will have something to be able to get it; there does not seem to be any sense that there is a nature of things which may disappoint the most thoroughly organised and disciplined self-will in the world. You seem to

---

[1] *The Holy Spirit in Faith and Experience,* by Professor A. Lewis Humphries, M.A.

[2] *London Theological Studies,* by Members of the Faculty of Theology in the University of London.

think the repeal of the Trades Disputes Acts impossible, but if it is not repealed it will have to be circumvented somehow, for its practical effect is to legalise every violence in a strike short of murder. It simply suspends the law where there is a trade dispute, and I don't believe any society in the world can exist on that footing. Government by soldiers is the worst government ever invented, but it is better than none, and if it is forced upon the nation by sheer lawlessness even the lawless will have to accept it. But you may think I am turning Tory or timorous if I write like this, which I hope is not the case.

15 LILYBANK GARDENS, GLASGOW, W.,
*March* 29, 1912.

I enclose one or two more reviews: I have never read so screamy a book as the *Renascence of Faith.*[1] The man should be sentenced to read nothing but Horace for six months; it is a pity so right-hearted a person should be lost for want of knowledge and of self-control. His language in places is simply awful, yet he is a Presbyterian minister apparently.

I am sorry to see you so severe on Asquith. As far as I can make out, he is absolutely right both about the strike and the Suffrage business, and unless I am much mistaken the event will prove

[1] *The Renascence of Faith,* by Richard Roberts.

so.  To have put figures into the Bill would have been to admit that Parliament can fix wages, and that it ought to do so ; but it can no more fix wages than it can fix the amount of sunshine there is to be next year, and I am thankful that the House of Commons stood by him in forcing this patent fact on the minority.  It *is* a fact, and to deny it just to save the face of the Miners' Federation would have been a mistake in every point of view.  No doubt the fight for better terms will be resumed whenever the miners think they are prepared, but in the nature of things it is an endless fight ; it is going on all the time, and would go on all the same no matter what figures were in a bill.  The miners have got a complete victory as it is—but one which practically implies compulsory arbitration.

15 LILYBANK GARDENS, GLASGOW, W.,
*April* 6, 1912.

W. P. Paterson told me some time ago that the Established Church was going to take a momentous step, which meant literally taking their life in their hand.  They have done it, and no mistake, in their newly published document.  It is just possible that they have taken our life in their hand too.  As far as I can make out, it is a frank admission that the Claim of Right was justified, and that the

Free Church in 1843 chose the good part; and it is an offer to meet us still on that basis. Whether it is anything more I am not quite clear; and in spite of the last sentence I am not clear whether it forgoes privilege as unambiguously as it proposes to seek (perhaps to assert) liberty. But it creates a kind of responsibility for all Christians in Scotland such as has not been put on them in this region of duty for a very long time.

Thanks for sending me Bury and Thumb: I am sure to learn a lot from both.

15 LILYBANK GARDENS, GLASGOW, W.,
*April* 12, 1912.

I was on the point of writing you about the Established Church proposals when your letter came. Of their general character I think as you do; they go far beyond anything I could have anticipated, and they put the Church of Scotland in a very favourable position in the eyes of the public. There is only one point in regard to which I would anticipate very serious trouble. In § 2 on page 1 they say, ' In the Joint Report submitted to the Assembly of 1911 the view was indicated that it would be difficult if not impracticable to secure concurrence in any attempt to define special State relations in a modern statute,' etc. This view was only indicated in the

Church of Scotland part of the Joint Report; and the inference drawn from it, that ' in this connection legislation would probably have to be limited to the recognition by Parliament of the freedom which must be a condition of any possible union, and the repeal in general terms of all enactments in any way inconsistent there- with,' would certainly not be accepted by a considerable part of our Church. For what it means is simply this : there may be and must be legislation extending the Church's liberty, but it can only be in such a form as leaves its politi- cal status unaffected. This, I say, will not be acceptable. The main causes that keep the Churches apart are two. The first is that the Church of Scotland does not possess something which we think indispensable—spiritual liberty : and the second is that the Church of Scotland does possess something which we regard as im- possible—political privilege. In these new pro- posals there is a satisfactory dealing with the first, but it is open to argument, to say the least, that the second is ignored or rather is tacitly reasserted. I asked W. P. Paterson before this document was drafted if it was an invitation to unite on the basis of the Claim of Right, and he said, ' Perhaps that is not very far off it.' But the Claim of Right was the claim of an Established Church : and in this document also, while liberty is to be attained, it is to be attained without compromising ' the claim of the United Church to recognition by the State as national,' etc. It must be very hard for those who have always prided themselves on it to resign the prestige of being *the* national establishment of religion, but there are great numbers in our Church who will never enter a Church which makes such a claim. That was what was in my mind when I spoke of the State, on State occasions, availing itself of the reunited Presbyterian Church as *representative* of the Christianity of the nation, not as *excluding* other Churches from the Christianity of Scotland ; and if the ' statutory disclaimer ' referred to in § 5, and the similar idea in § 11, could have this character definitely impressed upon them, I think for the average man the impediment would be overcome. When Christianity is represented on State occasions, as most people think it should be, then it should be represented in this country by the Presbyterian Church. I have no feelings about the relations of Church and State which make it difficult and embarrassing for me to say this ; and if this would content the other side, I venture to think it would content most men on ours.

About the endowments I have never been greatly interested. I would never lift a finger to see them taken from the Church of Scotland even if it remained in its present relation to the State. I have often been amused at the inconsistent way

in which Established Church men talked about
them in the Committee; in one breath they
would have it that they belonged to the Church,
not the State, and that for the State to touch them
was sacrilege; in the next, they were the State's
gift to the Church, and the most important part
of the national recognition of religion. But the
Church has had them long, and is entitled to
count on them, and I have no doubt they are
used as honourably and as beneficially for the
country as if they were handed over to some
Government department to squander. If they
were commuted, and on the assumption that they
were Church and not State property—though
held on a peculiar title—handed over to the
Church to be used at its discretion, or at least
with the same freedom with which it uses the
rest of its property, I should have no objection
to make. But I am not so sure of the immense
gain, though the amount is £220,000 per annum,
and not, as you say, twice in your letter, perhaps
by a slip of your typist, £120,000. The Church
of Scotland has many congregations in Glasgow,
endowed to the extent of £120 per annum, whose
ministers can hardly get more than this, and who,
even when supplemented from the Small Livings,
are far worse off than our unendowed city
ministers, none of whom (if they make even the
pretence of doing Home Mission work) have less
than £275, including clearance for house rent.

Carnegie Simpson seems to read the whole document in a sinister sense, as an attempt to get us
all into an established and endowed national
Church, but I think he is for once like Voltaire,
who had a great gift of seeing the devil when he
was not there.　Still, not only men like Barr and
J. A. Paterson and Benjamin Martin, but many
more, are deeply committed on the head of ' public
money,' and there are sure to be difficulties.
War with the Church of Scotland would be mad
and bad, but what of war within our own borders
—and me going to preach for the Central Fund in
U. P. churches both on Sunday first and the
Sunday following.

15 LILYBANK GARDENS, GLASGOW, W.,
*May* 2, 1912.

Herewith I send notices of Bury[1] and Thumb.[2]
The last is a complete mistake : they have translated the wrong book.　Thumb has an excellent
book on Greek in the Hellenistic age, most useful
to the large class of N. T. students, which has
philological interest; but I don't believe there are
ten people in this country who want so severely
scientific a book on such a scale about a mere
' vernacular ' which contains nothing worth
reading.　It took fifteen years to sell the first

[1] *History of the Eastern Roman Empire*, by Professor J. B. Bury.
[2] *Handbook of the Modern Greek Vernacular*, by Professor Albert
Thumb of Strassburg.

edition in Germany, and they will not sell the translation in 150.

I suppose you have seen the confused outbreak in Glasgow Presbytery about the memorandum. I knew that Orr had strong feelings about the memorandum, and if he expresses them in the Assembly, they will command attention. It is not only acrid extremists who scan the method of uniting the Churches with a certain suspicion, but men who are generously resolved never to be members in a Church which claims an exclusive privilege for itself, and men who are obstinately resolved never to abate an inch of their privilege. The *Herald* speaks to-day about the great concessions the Church of Scotland has made : I felt inclined to write and ask to have them enumerated. So far as I can make out the memorandum, the ' statutory dis-claimers ' suggested just amount to this : the Church of Scotland disclaims pronouncing other Christian denominations in Scotland to be no parts of the Catholic Church of Christ, but it still pronounces them to be no part of the national Christianity of Scotland. This is the nerve of the difficulty ; we are not going into any Church which makes the people with whom we have acted in Church and in public life Dissenters, and the memorandum (unless it can be modified) leaves this objectionable status unaffected. I will cer-tainly be on the side of peace, but I will not be on

the side of union unless more can be done than
has ever been suggested to meet just scruples on
this point. Yet I dread the consequences of
failure, and feel it would be a terrible condemnation of the Churches if there were not wisdom
and goodness in them to carry through what
has gone so far.

AIX-LA-CHAPELLE,
*June* 7, 1912.

I post with this an article for the *B. W.*[1]
I hope you have had a good holiday at
Brighton. I am here on the way to Eisenach;
this place has always had an attraction for my
mind, but I never visited it before. It is
very thriving and intensely Catholic, yet the
lies of the Catholic Church are more gross
and palpable in everything connected with the
Cathedral than they are in Rome itself. I don't
wonder at the mercilessness of the post-Reforma-
tion religious wars : I think I can understand
how creatures so different as those who believe
what is identified with religion here and those
who don't should feel that their adversaries had
no right to be, and that earth would be well rid
of them. Yet the streets swarm with children,
and yesterday was a holiday, and they all seemed
as happy as possible.

[1] ' God's Forgiveness and Ours.' (Leading article of June 13, 1912.)

15 Lilybank Gardens, Glasgow, W.,
*September 4, 1912.*

What a holiday you must have had! I hope it
has the compensation that you will enjoy getting
back to work again. The book of which I enclose a notice—the *Christian View of the World*[1]
—is rather a remarkable one in its way, but its
volubility is inconceivable. The flood of words
is like these Lammas floods—you want a cowl
to pull over your head and ears so as not to be
drenched and carried away by it. The more philosophy one reads, the more indispensable a sceptical
strain appears to give either reality or interest to
men's thoughts. It is all very well for God to be
omniscient, but a man who affects omniscience
or anything akin to it, even in the name of God,
is tiresome. I am going to preach in Dundee on
the Sunday at the Parish Church to the British
Association—or any of them that will come ; and
have got the essential provision of a good text.

The Manse of Dundee,
*September 9, 1912.*

I am posting the sermon with this,[2] but
you may be under a misapprehension, from
what appeared in the papers, as to its relation

---

[1] By Professor George John Blewett, Toronto.

[2] 'Christian Faith in God,' Dr. Denney's sermon preached at
Dundee, in connection with the meetings of the British Association.
This appeared as a leading article in the *British Weekly* of September
12, 1912.

to Schäfer. In point of fact it was finished some days before he spoke, and read exactly as it is written, and had no reference to him whatever. By chance or providence there are a few expressions in it which might be supposed to apply to his address, and that must be why the *Herald* says all the official preachers dealt with the President's views on life. I certainly did not, and in the circumstances would hardly have thought it becoming to take my text from Schäfer rather than from the New Testament. I have since had his address, and think it an astonishing illustration of how uneducated a man may be who is nevertheless in the front rank of a special science. It has shaken some of my heretical ideas about the proper training for ministers, and inclined me to the old belief that some philosophical education is indispensable. Schäfer is unphilosophical almost to the extent of being illiterate and in any generous sense unintelligent. But this is not matter for a sermon, and the matter of my sermon, as you will see, is worlds away from this.

15 Lilybank Gardens, Glasgow, W.,
*October* 4, 1912.

I enclose a notice of Frazer's last two volumes : [1] I don't like either the mental or the

[1] *Spirits of the Corn and of the Wild,* by J. G. Frazer, D.C.L.

spiritual quality of them any better as he goes on, and I should like to see them reviewed by a Christian Voltaire, if one could imagine such a combination. The way in which the haziest and most precarious hypothesis unconsciously turns into fact, and in which the highest things are insulted, not by being traced to their roots in things lower, but identified with the lowest to which they seem to present even faint or remote analogies, is beyond belief unless one reads the book through. The one truly praiseworthy thing in it is the immense and indomitable industry with which he accumulates everything relevant to his subject—not to speak of great masses of matter the relevance of which is to me entirely dubious.

We are getting under weigh here again. The College opens on Wednesday, and yesterday we had the first meeting for Conference with the Established Church. There will be some very tight places to get through before the union is accomplished, as I hope it will be ; for I do not think that many of the Church of Scotland people realise yet to what they have been committed by their own memorandum. Their action about Welsh Disestablishment—in Presbyteries—shows what their real feeling about a privileged Church is, and, unless privilege is extinguished, any one in our Church could defeat the Union. Orr, I know, is very suspicious about this, and any word or action of his carries great weight. I am sorry to say he is far from well.

I hope you are looking forward cheerfully to the winter, and feeling fit. Though I have lectured through 2 Corinthians in church, and read it with a class, I had to look up the Concordance for ' we are weak in him.' It is so good a text that I almost grudge you the discovery of it.

15 LILYBANK GARDENS, GLASGOW, W.,<br>
October 25, 1912.

Along with two or three notices of books, of which the most interesting is Hensley Henson's sermons,[1] I enclose the lecture I gave at the opening of the hall, which perhaps might suit *The Expositor*. It is at one or two points rather direct in form for an essay ; but if you consult at all for the general reader (Christian) as well as for the professional public who batten on Odes of Solomon, etc., you may be able to give it a place. I have read *Edwin Drood* to be able to appreciate your study, but your reviewer in the *B. W.* has let out your secret almost too completely. For a man who reads *Edwin Drood* for the first time it will be nearly impossible to get his mind outside of your

[1] *The Creed in the Pulpit*, by the Rev. Hensley Henson, D.D , Canon of Westminster (now Bishop of Durham).

solution. The story itself did not much impress me ; very little of it, I should say, is Dickens at his best, yet the best bits of it are as unmistakably Dickens as the best (and the worst) of Milton are indubitably his own.

The Home Rule Bill is going to make some trouble in our Church. Glasgow Presbytery refused to discuss a motion sympathising with the Irish Protestants, and a number of leading elders here are organising an attempt to get this decision reversed. There is a curious likeness between the Home Rule and the Church Union situation. It looks as if Ulster might defeat the one, and as if a resolute group of voluntaries might defeat the other. Possibly affairs in Turkey may soon absorb public interest so much that nobody will have a thought to spare for either. This is our first fog, which makes me hope you keep well.

15 LILYBANK GARDENS, GLASGOW, W.,
*November* 10, 1912.

I enclose the reviews I had : I thought you would be crowded out with this kind of matter at present. Ruffini's book [1] is quite interesting—as interesting as a book on religious liberty can be by a man who has no convictions in

---

[1] *Religious Liberty*, by Professor Francesco Ruffini of Turin, with a preface by J. B. Bury.

O

religion, and to whom liberty means the right
not to be bothered about such things; but
except as a repertory of facts it is not of much
use.   Still I have written about it at some
length, for we are certain to hear more of it.

We are likely, I think, to come to real business
about the memorandum now.  What you say
of the country in Aberdeenshire seems to be
pretty true everywhere, and is making an impression on people's minds, and there are corresponding facts in the towns—even in Glasgow,
which at the moment is on a springtide of pro-
sperity.  I had no real idea, till I began to be
interested in the Central Fund, with what difficulty many of our poorer churches get along.
I visited two this week with overdrafts on their
congregational account of £200 and £240 respec-
tively.  They can no more raise £200 than they
can raise £200,000, and they are paying their
ministers by sinking continually deeper in the
bog.  Apparently nobody can stop them, and
the banks give them money on the presumption
that the Church at large will pay rather than
allow a scandal.  Judging by much that one sees
and hears, I doubt if this presumption is as good
a security as it once was.  Anyhow, we have at
present more churches than can maintain themselves, and though consolidation always means
loss, it is the policy which seems to attract
meanwhile.  The one non-hopeful sign in the

union negotiations is the tendency to sniff at religious equality and to insist on a State recognition which will secure political prestige. If the Church of Scotland can learn to be Christian on this point, I believe everything else would be easy ; but if the article (*Scotsman*) on Ruffini's book on the morning the Conference met was inspired, as it is said to have been, there are storms ahead. I hope you are the better for Brighton, though how you can rest in a place where the motors stand four deep on Sunday I cannot imagine. Better even preach, as I have to do.

15 Lilybank Gardens, Glasgow, W.,
*November* 21, 1912.

It was very good of you to send me your book,[1] and I read it with great curiosity. As I have not read any other solution of the mystery, you may not think it of much consequence that it seemed very convincing to me, but it did. Of course it is useless to ask how Dickens would have finished the story, but I could imagine myself becoming more excited about that than about the one point who Datchery was, and what part he was to have in the working out of the sequel. If I knew who was going to write the next essay on the Odes of Solomon, I would send him a copy. The only

---

[1] *The Mystery of Edwin Drood*, by W. Robertson Nicoll.

really convincing thing that has been done on that is Bernard's Essay in the *Journal of Theol. Studies,* and I am going to read no more (unless by him) until I see some one thoroughly tackling this.

I liked Macaulay's sermons very much,[1] but how much because the man himself attracts and impresses me greatly I really cannot tell. They have the charm at least of being extremely like their author. I could wish he had done something else than sermons, as he is thoroughly capable of doing; I know no one with more power of thinking philosophically. They were ill advised when they would not have him at St. George's : he was the very man to maintain the best traditions of their church.

I hope to see Forsyth here in a week or two : he is coming to preach at the University. That is a very unexhilarating function to come so far from home for, but I hope he will get an audience. No one almost gets students, but the Archbishop of York got a crowd of the public. The Divorce Commission here strengthened the hands of the minority by asking too much : the majority report will suit the ecclesiastical, perhaps the Christian, party quite well. But the question is fearfully difficult, once you admit a question at all.

[1] *The Word of the Cross,* by A. B. Macaulay, M.A.

15 Lilybank Gardens, Glasgow, W.,
*November* 29, 1912.

The reviews of Deissmann [1] and Schweitzer [2] which I enclose were only possible for me this week because I had studied both already in the original. Deissmann is a man whose airs (and reputation) immensely exceed his merits, especially as a thinker, and Schweitzer's criticism of him is well deserved. The audacity of Schweitzer carries you over everything the first time, but there is as much cheek as wit in his book—which is often the case with people who deal in paradox.

15 Lilybank Gardens, Glasgow, W.,
*December* 19, 1912.

The enclosed observations on the Seven of Oxford [3] are perhaps too long for an article; if you think so, they will do as a long review. The book as a whole does not much impress me; the man I liked best through the writing was Temple, though there is a touch of donnishness and juvenility about them all. I have not said anything about Peggotty and Little Em'ly, though it is very funny. I remember in

[1] *St. Paul: a Study in Social and Religious History*, by Adolf Deissmann.

[2] *Paul and his Interpreters: a Critical History*, by Albert Schweitzer.

[3] *Foundations*. A leader on this book, by Dr. Denney, appeared in the *British Weekly* of December 24, 1912.

reading Moberly's father's book being struck by
the same want of reference to Macleod Campbell,
though neither of them has an idea which does
not come from that source. But what they all
want is a really serious study of New Testament
exegesis. It is too ridiculous for men to write
about the Christian religion from a great University, when they really could not pass a good
examination on the apostolic texts.

We finished our classes to-day for the Christmas holidays, and, like you, I am glad of the
break. We have just finished visiting all our
Presbytery in connection with the Central Fund,
and that too is a relief, as in the course of the visitation I have gone to thirty-six congregations
myself.

15 LILYBANK GARDENS, GLASGOW, W.,
*January* 17, 1913.

I was pleased to see you cursing the people
who take or send children out of church when
the sermon comes on. The whole truth in this
business is that children like to be—and will
be—where their fathers and mothers are. If
this is recognised, there is no problem of
the children : but if it is not, the problem is
insoluble. I will tell you a story of Spurgeon,
not for your competition, though you can
tell it anonymously if you like. I once heard

him read the third chapter of Daniel, about the
burning fiery furnace, etc. He read it a little
pompously, all about the harp, sackbut, psaltery,
etc., down to v. 7—' the golden image that
Nebuchadnezzar the king had set up.' Then he
made a little pause, and said with ironical emphasis on the last word, ' Church and State.'
Then he read on to the end where Nebuchadnezzar makes the contrary decree appointing the
fiery furnace for all who speak against the God
of the Hebrew children, and after another little
pause which created expectation, he said, ' Church
and State again—and *wrong every time.*' These
were the only comments he made in reading, but
he preached a powerful sermon on a text in the
same chapter which, like some other good things,
has disappeared in the Revised Version : ' *Is it
true*, O Shadrach, Meshach and Abednego,' etc.,
will you stick to it in face of the burning fiery
furnace ? It was a series of illustrations of the
things that rise up and challenge men when they
have taken a stand for God. I heard him once
do a delightfully inconsistent thing in preaching.
His text was ' Return, return, O Shulamite.'
He said he did not know whether the voice was
that of Christ calling to a backsliding Church, or
that of the old companions of the Church calling
her away from Christ : but to be sure of getting
the truth, he preached on it quite earnestly first
in the one sense, and then in the other !

15 LILYBANK GARDENS, GLASGOW, W.,
*March* 22, 1913.

I was extremely interested in your Mark Rutherford number, and even more in your letter than in the article. Nothing in his story seems to explain adequately his antipathy to evangelicalism; it seems to me pretty much another proof that literature is the work of the natural man, and that nonconforming self-conscious virtue is essentially repugnant to it. Of course such virtue is very liable to Pharisaism, and can be criticised by inspiration, but it is much more frequently caricatured from a lower level than corrected from a higher. Nobody seems to be good-humoured with it but Shakespeare. What an extraordinary thing that was you quoted from the *Westminster Review* advertisement of his Spinoza. It is one of the mysteries about him to me that he was fascinated by Spinoza, though his other favourite Wordsworth is in many of his greatest passages—in all his philosophy of nature—an unconscious Spinozist. We close next week, and I hope to send you soon a notice of von Hügel on *Eternal Life*.[1]

15 LILYBANK GARDENS, GLASGOW, W.,
*April* 4, 1913.

I have sent you an article on von Hügel.

[1] *Eternal Life: a Study of its Implications and Applications,* by Baron Friedrich von Hügel.

The book is not uninteresting, once you apply your mind to it, but I doubt if it will make much impression. The style in which it is written is simply incredible ; it is in no tongue of men or of angels, and yet there is an occasional pungency and even felicity about it that could only come from a very live mind. Somehow I never can learn from a Roman Catholic controversialist. They all have the complacency of infallibility about them, no matter how humbly they submit what they have written to the judgment of the Church ; they all claim the right not only to say everything, but everything else to the bargain, so that the total impression left in one's mind is that of dealing with a man whose one principle is Heads I win, tails you lose. Able and independent as he is, von Hügel in this respect is just like the rest. I am going from home to-morrow morning for a few days, so that if you want to print this for your next issue I am afraid I cannot read a proof ; but I have made any proper names in it quite plain, so it does not matter.

Our Union negotiations are certainly at a very critical, but I believe also a very hopeful stage. Our one chance of getting safely through is to leave off talking about words, and try whether we cannot agree about things and duties. Orr thinks those who are keen for union are trying to square the circle, and does not seem to see that

what he is trying to do is to circularise the square
—which is (I suppose) equally impossible.  Pray
for the health of Henderson if you pray for the
peace of Jerusalem.  Many thanks for what you
told me about the Antinomians.  I always find
it very hard to believe there could have been
such beings.

15 Lilybank Gardens, Glasgow, W.,<br>
July 9, 1913.

I have had these books a long time, but after
the Assembly I had a holiday, and have only
been able to get them done since I came
back.  There is nothing very new about any
of them.

You will be sorry to hear that Orr is very un-
well.  After the Assembly he went to Germany
with two of his sons, one of them luckily a doctor,
and came back in a very alarming condition.  I
saw him on Thursday last, when he had not had
his clothes off for a week : his heart affects his
breathing so that he cannot lie down nor get any
sufficient rest.  I hope he will get safely over it
yet, but it is impossible not to be anxious.

The Society for Biblical Study which was here
lately does not seem to be a very serious affair.
I had Lake staying with me, and much as I dislike his opinions I took to the man very much.
He said my review in the *British Weekly* was the
only serious review his book had had : lots of

notices, mostly laudatory, but mostly also (he said) by people who obviously knew nothing about the matter. He has a new edition coming out soon. Almost the best thing in the proceedings was a paper read by Mr. George Smith of Merchiston Castle School on teaching the Bible in schools like his. It struck me as having all kinds of good qualities. Charles, the apocalyptic man, ended a paper on ' reinterpretation and comprehension ' by a wildly irrelevant and absurd defence of Church Establishments. I should have liked to hear your friend Lathbury upon it. As for our Church question, although I have good hopes of it, I cannot but feel that all our troubles are still ahead of us : I am astonished to find how unenthusiastic and even suspicious great numbers of our best people are.

15 LILYBANK GARDENS, GLASGOW, W.,
*September 7, 1913.*

I enclose something about Dr. Orr, which I hope will be in quantity and intention something like what you wish. I had a great affection for him, and will miss him more than I can say. He had been failing for a good while, and especially for a year past was not quite himself ; but he was a big man by the grace of nature and of the Gospel too, and his removal makes a great void.

15 LILYBANK GARDENS, GLASGOW, W.,
*September* 18, 1913.

I enclose notices of two books you sent me.
There is a kind of interest in both, but,
though both are modern, neither is up to
date. Kent's is an eminent example of a
man so full of his own mind that he sees little
in the Gospels but what he brings, and therefore
not only misses what is there, but finds
a great deal which isn't. In spite of its moral
earnestness, I cannot take it as a favourable
symptom of the influence of Yale on American
Christianity.

I am living just now in an atmosphere of conferences about the Central Fund, designed to
impress people who are not very much interested
in the Christian religion. Though there is a great
deal of good will in the Church, there is not much
enthusiasm, and what there is is mainly congregational. The necessity of the Church to the
maintenance of the Christian faith is not felt by
some, and the necessity of the Christian faith
itself is not strong conviction with others. We
are again going to have small classes at the College, and if things do not take a turn we will soon
have neither men nor money. That union with
the Church of Scotland, though it seems to me a
clear duty to attempt it, will strengthen the
Church in the country, I do not see : what it
needs is to be spiritually strengthened, not

politically or financially, and meanwhile we seem to have lost contact with the source of power. I feel pretty sure also that we will have to make great changes both in the way of finding and of training ministers.   Much of our work in the hall is doubly irrelevant ; it is unsuitable for the men we get, and it is no preparation for their work.

15 LILYBANK GARDENS, GLASGOW, W.,
*September* 22, 1913.

I am just starting for the train to attend a Central Fund Committee in Edinburgh, but take a moment to thank you for your letter just received.   Please amend the ' worthless legend ' sentence at your discretion.   I would not have said it except that I felt provoked by Kent's referring to this 'priceless story' as the only thing of real historical value in the Fourth Gospel.   Ever since I read the amazing page upon it in *Ecce Homo*, I have had my doubts about it, and I am more than ever inclined to think that Wellhausen is right in describing it as ' ganz apocryph.'   But that is no reason for hurting anybody's feelings about it, especially the feelings of ' one of these little ones.'

I had two or three letters from people about the reference I made to Moulton's views on the Australian and New Zealand military training —one from Mr. Ford, who was Chairman of the

Congregational Union two years ago, enclosing a cutting with what he thought a very convincing and I an extremely absurd letter from a Melbourne minister about it. Most of the people who go in for Norman Angell seem to overlook the fact that Norman Angell himself expressly declares that while the present mind of the world is what it is he would not abate in the slightest the present measures for the defence of the nation against attack.

I cannot thank you enough for what you say about the *British Weekly* and the Central Fund, and I will write about it soon : your help will be of the greatest value.

15 LILYBANK GARDENS, GLASGOW, W.,
*October* 4, 1913.

I enclose a few notices of books. The one on the *Preaching of Islam* [1] I had written before I got your note about the scale on which you wished them done, but it is really a standard book, and deserves more than the space I have given it. I have compressed the others as much as possible, but may do better with practice, even though I never attain to the vanishing point illustrated in your ' Short Notices ' this week. I felt a little doubtful how

---

[1] *The Preaching of Islam: a History of the Propagation of the Muslim Faith,* by Professor T. W. Arnold, C.I.E.

I should treat Winstanley.   Here is a competent
enough book on an important subject, but it
could easily have been put into a third of its
bulk without losing a fact or an idea, and it
is execrably written—interminable sentences with
neither structure nor relief about them, and no
sense of proportion.   It seems incredible that
any educated man should be capable of writing
so badly.

You know very much better than I how the
*B. W.* can help the Central Fund, and I know
your interest in it.   Next Friday we are to have
a meeting in the Assembly Hall : if your Edinburgh correspondent could send you a good
report of that, I believe it would be useful.   The
idea is to interest the younger men in the Church :
the enclosed cutting from the *Record* gives the
programme.   Any time you wish to write, I will
be happy to get you the latest facts and figures.
I wish I knew exactly what you refer to when
you say that the management of the fund has
not been satisfactory for some years at least.   It
has not been in existence quite five years, and the
superficial complexities due to the fact that it is
an amalgamation of two previously existing
systems, and not a brand new thing, have caused
an immense amount of misunderstanding and
prejudice, and occasionally a little friction ; but
as far as I can make out, it is getting to be understood and accepted, and the tendency to shrink

is unhappily not peculiar to it. It is common to all our funds, and I fear to the Church itself. This session we have only thirty-seven students entering our three halls, and the reason men are not becoming ministers—the glaring reason which no one refers to—is that they are not becoming members of the Church at all. I often feel when I speak of the Central Fund like a man trying to get a pot to boil by stirring it, when what is really required is somebody to mend the fire. However, it takes everybody and everything, and I mean to do what I can in this job, and hope the fire will be fed with fresh fuel.

I was very much interested in your letter on Stead. I only once was in his company—in Lindsay's—where he sprawled on a sofa and talked of the Pope and the Czar, the German Emperor and Chamberlain. That he should be a good hater was what one would have expected, but I was amazed at what you said of his vindictiveness.

15 LILYBANK GARDENS, GLASGOW, W.,
*October* 31, 1913.

It was very good of you to give two columns of the *British Weekly* to the Central Fund, and I am sure it will do good. I agree entirely about what you say about the Emergency Fund, the Foreign Mission Fund, etc. ; the one reason why the C. F. does not prosper is because people are not interested in it.   But there are some matters of fact in the article about which I believe there are misapprehensions.   For instance, when it is said that ' the generous appeal of the Sustentation Fund as a fund for the support of religion in Scotland raised a generation ago from the 300,000 members of the then Free Church a sum only 28 per cent. less in amount than that raised by the 500,000 members of the United Free Church under the new regulations, which secure by promise a certain minimum payment to the fund,' the facts are exactly the reverse of what is stated.   It was the old regulations of the Sustentation Fund that required congregations to promise a minimum, whereas under the new regulations of the Central Fund there is no such requirement, and the calling of ministers is sanctioned often in congregations which make no promise, except that they will do their best for the fund.   Often, also, where a minimum is indicated, it is understood to be nominal.

For example, the Church in which I am a member, put down £600, but has always given from £870 to £900 ; and Kelvinside, after indicating a minimum of £800, has regularly given over £1200.  Wellington, again, a U. P. congregation giving about £1200, simply refuses to promise anything at all.  Congregations which

P

require to be helped by the fund, are asked to tell what they can give for themselves, which I do not think is unreasonable, and it is not at all in connection with them that the decline has taken place. Personally, I have always argued on the line of your article, and when the quinquennial revision was to take place two years ago I got the Committee, instead of sending out schedules to be filled up with definite promises tending to stereotype congregational giving, to make an intimation that we depended on all congregations doing their best for the common cause, and that meanwhile we would presume that they would not fall short of the average givings for the last three years.

I have an impression, though I admit it rests as yet on rather vague grounds, that we are going to improve ; but it may be more slowly than we would like. I am not sure that your article is right when it thinks we might succeed if we enlisted the active and energetic sympathy of women. The weakness in the whole business is that it has not the sympathy of men. It is men who have the money, and who could make up for all we have lost ; but they are indifferent to the Church even when they have not left it. There are members of our Church in Glasgow who have motor cars and steam yachts and give less to the C. F. than their ministers do. The contrast of Glasgow and Edinburgh has been in my mind ever since I had anything to do with this business, but I do not understand what your article says about it. It has been practically what it is at all times and under all regulations or absence of regulations, and I can only explain it by supposing that Edinburgh, partly as the seat of the Assembly and the headquarters of Church business, has always been a churchier place than Glasgow ; partly also because there is nothing in Edinburgh like the United Evangelistic Association here, which is mainly supported by members of our Church, some of whom literally spend thousands a year upon it, while they frankly say they are not interested in the C. F. ; partly perhaps because Edinburgh is more of a village than Glasgow, and the Church has a relatively bigger place in its interests. The last three paragraphs of the article I agree with unreservedly : I have tried to rub them in wherever I go. It is no use badgering the poor congregations ; it is not congregations at all which have to be dealt with, but individuals. The individuals I find most impracticable are well-off people who say there are too many churches—that country ministers have far too little to do, and don't do it—that there is not £200 worth of work in a great many parishes—and that if people who did their work as these people do it were in our offices they would not be there a week. I am not imagining these things : they have all been said to me, and, though it is not easy to argue about them in public, they are present in many people's minds. But I did not mean to bore you when I began, but to thank you sincerely, as I do, for your help. I am going to-morrow to Dumfries to speak about it, and on Friday to Aberdeen, and will try to find the right way of putting the case to sympathetic and indifferent souls alike.

I enclose two reviews. The Cambridge History is a terrible book. It is like being shown through the Co-operative Stores. There is everything in it you want, and everything you don't want, and an impression from which you cannot get away that the whole thing comes short somehow of being first class.

15 LILYBANK GARDENS, GLASGOW, W.,
*November* 18, 1913.

I ought to have written you long ago to thank you for *A Bookman's Letters*, but put off till I could send this notice of MacEwen's history. The *Letters* are a truly delightful book, and it was very good of you to send me one. Unluckily for me, I am one of those who have never learned to read—this book of MacEwen's, though it interested me much, took me an unconscionable time to get through ; but I remember most of your letters, and the interest does not diminish but revives when I read them again. I don't know whether you think it paradoxical to say so, but though I have never learned to read like you and Moffatt, I am really fond of reading, and have had, and still have, immense pleasure in it. MacEwen's is really a first-rate book,[1] and ought to be of great value to our Church and country for a generation to come. It could not have the opulence of Lindsay's *Reformation*, but it must be a new light for almost every one, and if the second volume is as good as the first, it will be a great classic. There is no strikingly good writing in it, certainly no purple patches ; but most of it is admirably expressed, and there are occasional felicities, especially of a quietly argumentative kind. There is a very good reply to Andrew Lang on Knox's lack of appreciation for things in Romish religion—which in the Romish religion of Knox's time were simply not there. We had not a very good meeting for the Central Fund in Aberdeen—at least the attendance was not very good. But they said it was representative, and Smith spoke with his accustomed glow. I am a little hopeful in spite of the people who pour cold water on everything and are sure that everything you do will do more harm than good. The last thing the professional mourners are adding to their stock in trade is the assertion that

[1] *A History of the Church in Scotland,* by Rev. Professor A. R. MacEwen, D.D.

there are no people with money left in our Church ; they have all been driven out by our politics !

I am very much interested in what you told me of the surplus under the old Sustentation Fund; I had suspected something of the sort in isolated cases, but had no means of knowing whether it was common. The shortest way of putting the difference between the Sustentation Fund and the Central Fund, is to say that under the Central Fund all congregations in which the stipend amounts to £200 must be self-sustaining, and do not share in any surplus. If they pay their ministers up to £160 *through* the Fund—and they cannot pay them more than that in this way—then they must send at least £160 in. If they send less, they only get back what they send ; in no circumstances are they allowed to *profit* by the C. F. This is a point on which I have found some difficulty in getting people born and bred in the Sustentation Fund to be as intelligent as could be desired ; but it is *the* differentia of the new fund as opposed to the old. It is just another way of putting it, though not a very palatable way either to some people, to say that the regulations under which we work have turned the Sustentation Fund into an Augmentation Fund. It does two things only : (1) It raises to £160, not all congregations, but all who cannot provide that sum for themselves; (2) It distributes any surplus over and above what is required for this purpose, among Churches where the stipend is under £200. The old Free Church surplus was given according to merit ; all churches shared in it in proportion to their givings per member. The new C. F. surplus is given according to need ; only churches under £200 share in it, and the less they have otherwise the bigger their share. If a church with £160 gets £10 of surplus, one with £180 gets £5, and one with £190 gets £2, 10s.

I wish I could agree with you that we could easily raise £100,000 for endowment. At this moment I cannot think it practicable. Endowment contemplates a situation which is comparatively stable, and most people, I think, are impressed by the instability of our present position—especially of our present relation to the Church of Scotland. They want to know what is to become of the existing endowments before they furnish new ones. I am sure the C. F. suffers from this, unreasonable as it may be ; but I am equally sure, though I have nothing very palpable to go upon, that interest in it is being awakened, and I am not alarmed about the immediate future.

I am convinced that a great deal of the criticism of the rules is simply due to the fact that the fund has not been successful. If there were a revival of religion and of liberality, and if we could pay all our ministers £200 a year, the rules would be good enough; at least nobody would find fault with them. I am learning to be mightily patient, and to give the soft answer, which is by no means natural to me, to all the perplexed souls who want to understand elementary addition and subtraction.

15 LILYBANK GARDENS, GLASGOW, W.,
*January* 19, 1914.

I had hoped to send you some reviews sooner, but I have been preoccupied somehow, and only send this on Frazer now.[1] Surely no man ever had a mind so full of facts and so void of ideas. I am amused by a page in which he makes much use of ' the acute and learned Movers.' On the next page he quotes Robertson Smith. I never saw Smith's writing but once, in a letter Jebb showed me about something in the *Journal of Hellenic Studies*, but there he quoted the same work from which Frazer quotes, and referred to the author as ' the muddle-headed Movers.' I should like to know how Moulton finds Frazer's acquaintance a liberal

[1] *The Scapegoat*, by Dr. J. G. Frazer.

education, but perhaps I have what Lord Morley calls the intellectual fault of pugnacity. The Central Fund is not to be so good as I expected, though the congregations are up £2775.

15 LILYBANK GARDENS, GLASGOW, W.,<br>
February 12, 1914.

I hope you have had a good holiday on the Riviera. As you would see, I wrote a leader on the subject of Kennedy's book, but more on Inge than on him. Kennedy's is an excellent book, but it is all detail, and, though I have read it twice, I could not go into any detailed criticism in the *B. W.*[1] But I hope it will sell well, for of all subjects on which confident nonsense is talked, commend me to the ancient mysteries. This man whose book I enclose a notice of is of no real importance, but the subject is another of those on which a great deal is written with terribly little sense of its religious consequence, so I have given him rather more space than I would otherwise have done.

I don't know whether any one will send you any notice of my old friend and class fellow, A. D. Grant, who fell down dead at his own door in Greenock a fortnight ago. He was one of the best men I ever knew, an example of Christian

---

[1] *St. Paul and the Mystery Religions*, by Professor H. A. A. Kennedy, D.D. Dr. Denney's article appeared in the *British Weekly* of January 29, 1914.

goodness through and through, and at his funeral —he had been in the same church in Greenock about thirty years—the crowds lined the streets as if it had been the funeral of a king. I have not seen anything for long which showed so clearly what a power a truly Christian minister is who gives a lifetime to his work in one place. He had very remarkable gifts of other kinds also— knew English literature very well, and had read a great deal in French. The three men with whom I was most intimate in my year are all gone now.

15 LILYBANK GARDENS, GLASGOW, W.,
*March* 14, 1914.

I am sending with this a notice of the last two volumes of *The Golden Bough*,[1] and also a few lines on a volume of sermons by Campbell Moody,[2] which you did not send me, but which were given me by his brother. I knew Campbell Moody when he was a student —indeed he succeeded me, though not immediately, as missionary in St. John's Church here —and after a year or two he went to Formosa. He was there, I think, about fifteen years, and was a most devoted missionary, but for the last four years he has been in New Zealand—his

[1] By Dr. J. G. Frazer.
[2] *Love's Long Campaign*, by Rev. Campbell N. Moody, M.A.

wife had a tendency to consumption, and the soaking moist heat of Formosa was proving fatal to her.

We are getting near the end of our session now, and I am thankful, for I have found the Central Fund a distracting and time-consuming business. It is not so much that it adds to one's work, for when you do one thing you are not doing another, but somehow the feeling of responsibility for them both, even if you are neglecting one, becomes exhausting. However, I don't think it will be so bad next year; I have got the hang of it now, and can both understand things more quickly, and tell more quickly what is not worth thinking about.


15 LILYBANK GARDENS, GLASGOW, W.,
*March 25, 1914.*

Here are a few lines about Shebbeare,[1] who has tackled with some pedantry a business much too big for him.

What a frightful mess the Government have got into now! Whoever is responsible seems to have put them in the wrong every way the matter can be looked at, and though the indignation in the House of Commons against the action of the army will no doubt be echoed outside, it may be overborne by the feeling that people capable of

[1] *Religion in an Age of Doubt,* by the Rev. Charles Shebbeare, M.A.

such wanton mismanagement of their own interests are not fit to be trusted with the management of the nation's. If the Parliament Act is lost and everything else along with it, Churchill and Lloyd George may be never so eloquent but they will not be trusted again for a very long time.

15 LILYBANK GARDENS, GLASGOW, W.,
*April* 16, 1914.

I am beginning to be a little tired of seeing the same straw thrashed so often over Galatia, but as I am going to read Galatians with a class next winter I will take Watkins' [1] book as seriously as I can. The two books of which I enclose notices are quite interesting, but neither is of very high quality. Widgery is evidently a young man in a hurry who has much undigested reading floating about in his brain, and is capable of the most appalling mistakes in translating ; and Eucken [2] is what he is in all his recent books—copious, impalpable, and assured. His first big books were by far the best ; the recent ones have been degenerating into sermons by a superior person, and do not seem to me very likely to impress either ordinary sinners or serious thinkers.

[1] *St. Paul's Fight for Galatia,* by Rev. C. H. Watkins, M.A.
[2] *Can we still be Christians?* by Rudolf Eucken, translated by Lucy Judge Gibson.

15 Lilybank Gardens, Glasgow, W.,
*April* 20, 1914.

I have read this book of Watkins [1] with much interest. His historical conclusions seem to me on the whole quite sound, but he does not sufficiently understand that the true religion must be uncompromising. He has a very amusing footnote in which he seems to think he has disposed of Paul's anathema by the suggestion that it might possibly apply even to ourselves—and as if none of *us*—people of quality —could conceivably be damned ! To any one who is familiar with J. Weiss it was superfluous to name his teacher : Weiss is written all over it. The ' methodical ' precision of it is absurd, as indeed most exhibitions of the same kind are ; it refreshed me lately to see Harnack denounce them as pure waste of time.

15 Lilybank Gardens, Glasgow, W.,
*May* 11, 1914.

I was glad to see you speak so plainly about the ' provocative and wrecking ' minority report of the Church of Scotland Committee. The hostile party in the Church have forced the Committee to send the constitution to their Presbyteries at the same time at which it is sent to us, which puts us in an impossible position. What can we do with

[1] See *ante.*

it, when the Church of Scotland Presbyteries may throw it overboard ?   I have not seen any of our people yet, and do not know what Henderson has in mind, but everything looks less favourable than it did a year ago.   Yet with more Christianity in both Churches it should be impossible to fail.

15 Lilybank Gardens, Glasgow, W.,
*June* 27, 1914.

I put off reading this book of Alexander's because the man, somehow, did not impress me much when he lectured in our college, but I must have done him an injustice then.   It is really an excellent book, full of knowledge and of what is on the whole sound criticism ; and though it is wanting in brightness, there are here and there very good sentences in it.

I have been reading your articles on ' The Difference Christ makes ' with much interest.   The hopeful thing in our present situation is that everybody's conscience is on the same side as to the end to be aimed at : where people differ is as to the means.   This is not a question which conscience can settle, though people who are very much in earnest about the end are apt to accuse those who differ from them about the means, of having no conscience.

Lloyd George's intention to benefit the poor is

unquestionable, but though I do not grudge my share of the income tax, I think it is a fair question whether the increase of the income tax and the spending of it as it is spent does nothing but benefit the poor. And there is always the further trouble that when we claim justice for ourselves, we act as judges in our own cause and almost inevitably claim more. Just because democracy is omnipotent, it would need to be composed of unusually good men if it is to produce an unusually good and just Government. One of the things that has never been out of my mind since I went to Broughty Ferry and got £400 a year, is that my father worked from six in the morning till six at night, and often longer, from the time he was twelve till he died at seventy-two, never had a month's holiday in his life, and never made a seventh or an eighth of my income, though he was in every sense of the term as good a man as I am. The distribution of the rewards of labour between us was absurd, and I long to see it corrected, but I have no conviction that the minimum wage, and the right to work, and in short any legislation that has yet been conceived, is likely to do much in that direction. Nobody in Glasgow now works for the Corporation for less than 27s. a week ; but that wage is provided by rates paid by people many of whom have far less. I suppose they feel their prospects improved when any of their class benefit.

As it happens, I am going for my holidays this year also about the middle of August, but if you can tell me the dates for which the articles are wanted, I will see that they are at the office in good time. Indeed I could send them by August 10, and August 17, and save you any further trouble, as that would be soon enough for the first two weeks of your absence.

The Central Fund is apt to fall into a state of suspended animation this month and next, but the unconsciousness, I think, is not quite so profound as it has sometimes been. The association had increased nearly £2000 at the end of June—*i.e.* in six months—which is so far encouraging. If you have not seen the report, you may be interested by the statement on p. 8. It is contributions like your own additional £20 to which we owed £19,775 in the last five years, and every effort is being made—of course it has to be made privately—to have these continued. Last year they came to over £2700, and this year they are already over £2000. At this moment we are suffering somewhat from the political crisis. Lee, or rather his Highland Convener Martin, has found some of his ordinary supporters extremely crusty, and there is a donation of £1000, which has been regularly given to the Central Fund for years, at present in suspense for political reasons, or, as I should say, for political unreason. It is very good of you to be so faithful.

Talking of politics, I wish I could see half an inch into the fog. When all parties to the Conference admit that they can agree neither in principle nor in detail as to what should be done, the only inference is that somebody must be coerced. You say it must not be Ulster—probably you would say also it cannot be the Nationalists : all that remains is that it must be the Government and the Liberal party. *They* are to be coerced into dropping Home Rule, appealing to the country, and sacrificing the Parliament Act and all its natural or possible fruits. I could not imagine anything which would create a deeper feeling of resentment and disgust in all who have ever supported them. If the House of Lords reject the Amending Bill, as they will no doubt do, I see no course for the Government but to pass the Home Rule Bill without it, and take the responsibility of maintaining the King's Government in Ireland meantime, whatever the ' provisional ' government may do. If they simply cave in to the tempest of bad passions that has disgraced Christianity in the north of Ireland for two years past, they will never be forgiven. Though Asquith made the worst mistake of his career in passing that sentence about ' the cry of civil war,' he is so much abler than anybody on the opposite side that I still pin my faith to him,

Q

and even if he should be beaten at last I should not think it owing to the strength of the Opposition, but to some incurable perversity in the nature of things.

I do condole with you on losing a friend and helper of twenty years' standing : it must be impossible almost to replace her. But ' for this cause shall a man, or a woman leave ' even what one might think best worth keeping. I hope you have had prevision of the event, and some one in training.

*P.S.*—Have you seen Gwatkin's reply to Gore ? That is the best thing which has appeared in this controversy. I thought Jones in *The Expositor* tedious and artificial. Souter's short notes at the end struck me as the best thing in that number.

15 LILYBANK GARDENS, GLASGOW, W.,
*November* 24, 1914.

I send you notices of these two books. It is not so much that I dissent from all —— is saying, but his way of delivering his mind seems so fantastic and overstrained. No wonder men have nervous breakdowns if they have to preach in this unnatural high-falutin fashion all the time. Why doesn't he sit down and speak the word to them sometimes as Jesus did ? It is all about Jesus, but nothing could be less like the manner of the Gospels.

I don't know how you feel it—or rather I do—but I cannot think of anything but one, and feel it very hard to get any continuous work done either by myself or by my class. Last night we had the Annual Foreign Mission meeting in Glasgow, which is usually the event of our Church year. It was quite flat, and as much from the state of mind in the audience as from the speeches. Everybody was preoccupied. You felt that there was nothing in the speeches that had accumulated and represented any depth of thought or feeling ; men had just raked up anything that was lying about ; their interest was elsewhere. And yet one wishes there was more interest elsewhere than there is. I go with you heartily in every word you have written about recruiting. I can't make out some things at all, but I believe among the working classes here there is a widely diffused expectation that service will be made compulsory, and willingness to accept that when it is declared necessary as the just way of dealing with a national crisis, and a reluctance to give up good wages (for most men here are well employed) till the necessity is made apparent by the compulsion. Why the Government conceal the figures I cannot imagine, but well as they have done in the main I feel sure the nation is hungering for a little more success than we have yet had, and that their popularity will suffer heavily if there is not a decided change in Flanders soon. Yet what a burden they bear.

15 LILYBANK GARDENS, GLASGOW, W.,
*December* 5, 1914.

Many thanks for your most interesting letter. The new hand was unfamiliar to me, and as a ' grave nature, led by custom and therefore constant,' I could not help condoling with you a little on the loss of your old secretary. As it happened, I had read Macgregor's book [1]— I have been lecturing this winter on Galatians —and could write on it conveniently enough. There is no particular relevance in it to the war, though if any book was ever a stroke in a battle, Galatians is.

I am sorry to say that the apprehension I had about the arrest of the increase in the Central Fund in October has been verified. The congregations had gone up every month from the beginning of the year till the increase had reached £2692, but in November they have gone back about £1600, and the increase from this source is now only £1100. I have written something explaining the facts, and have asked Lee, who is

---

[1] *Christian Freedom:* the Baird Lecture for 1913, by Rev. W. M. Macgregor, D.D. Dr. Denney's article on this work appeared in the *British Weekly* of December 24, 1914.

typing some copies of it, to send one to you on Monday. I know your interest in the cause, and if you could give a place to it, or the most necessary part of it, in your Scotch edition, it would render us a real service. I shall have to speak of it in our Presbytery here on Tuesday, so that it could appear naturally as news in your next issue.

I hope you have good news from your son and son-in-law at the front. People like me are practically out of it, and can only feel how vain what we call sympathy is. Dr. Reith read last Sunday morning the names of seven young fellows from our congregation who are now in the fighting line—one his youngest son, John, who is in Armentières. It was almost too much for him.

15 Lilybank Gardens, Glasgow, W.,
*March* 8, 1915.

I know you are much in favour of the Government taking some drastic action about the use of liquor during the war. A memorial to the Prime Minister is being promoted here to stop the sale of distilled liquors in Scotland during the war, and is having extraordinary support. Every one to whom it is submitted seems willing to sign it—especially employers of labour, irrespective of party connections. I don't believe it is too much to say that if the country were polled it would be as unanimously and enthusiastically in favour of this measure as of the prosecution of the war itself. If you can do anything—as I am sure you can do much—to promote so good an object, you will earn the gratitude of every one who loves his country. I am sending with this a pamphlet by one of our University men and by Frank Knight, our minister (Dr. Reith's colleague): they are both very keen about it. There was some talk of having Lloyd George here on a Sunday, but I am not anxious for that. We don't want any more speeches, nor assurances that the Government will exercise its influence, etc., etc.; the only use of a Government is that in defiance of all influence it can put into Act legal powers; and if it is not willing to do this and do it soon, our Government is missing the day of its visitation.

I am sorry I have not been able to send you anything for *The Expositor*, but without being busier than usual, or at any rate without doing more than usual, I have somehow been unusually distracted. I will try some time soon.

15 Lilybank Gardens, Glasgow, W.,
*March* 12, 1915.

I was delighted to read your pronounce-ment on drinking and racing: it could not have been more effectively done, nor put on more unimpeachable ground, and I am sure all right-minded people are grateful to you. What is the matter with the *Glasgow Herald* in this connection I cannot tell, but they are thirled to the publicans somehow. The publicans are organised too, in view of 1920, as they have never been before ; and I believe they are in mortal terror that if we saw what like this country was for six months without whisky they would never get a look in again.

We hear it said that Bonar Law is strongly on the right side, but that Balfour is mightily non-committal, and we know what to expect from Younger. I have no hope of an agreed measure, but I believe the Government is quite strong enough to defy any interested opposition, if it had even a pennyworth of moral courage.

Moffatt's chances for the Professorship seem rising ; he had the best vote in our Presbytery, and I believe Fairweather's supporters will in the main give their second votes to him. But it is very difficult to calculate. Watt had a start, Lindsay's appreciation of him is known, and in some quarters the Historical New Testament is counted to its author for anything but righteousness still.

15 LILYBANK GARDENS, GLASGOW, W.,
*May* 27, 1915.

Your telegram did me good, and if anything could make one happy in such an
unhappy time it would be the discovery of
such an amount of unmerited goodwill as I
have experienced in the last few days. I need
not say that I was much more interested in
the election to the Church History Chair than in
my own, nor that Moffatt's appointment gave me
the liveliest pleasure. If only we could be sure
of having any students next year—or sure that
we ought to have any—we could think of the
future cheerfully. The neglected sins of the
nation are finding it out fearfully, and the Church
cannot escape.

MacEwen has made a most interesting Moderator—a little professorial, with a touch of the
academic disciplinarian, and a disposition to take
part in the procession as well as to look on from
the window. But he did everything with all his
heart and strength and mind, and, though I don't
agree with all his opinions and always feel a kind
of instability in his mental action, he spoke in
both his opening and closing addresses with
unusual and unmistakable spiritual power, and
every one was greatly impressed.

One of the most promising phenomena of the
week was the appearance of Freeland Barbour

in the Union discussion. He spoke with real distinction—intellectually I mean—and he has the art of saying just enough to be impressive without the fault, which preaching seems to induce, of iterating and urging when the moment for impressing is past. I don't know whether the solemnity of the whole circumstances damped the spirits of youth, but it seemed to me as if the business was left even more than usual in the hands of elderly men. I hope you keep well through all the horrors of the time.

15 Lilybank Gardens, Glasgow, W.,<br>
*July* 18, 1915.

It seems an age since I had any communication with you, and my conscience smites me that I have not been able to send you anything for *The Expositor*. I don't know whether other men are getting new light on the New Testament at present, but I do not feel as if I were. The interest of this commentary of McNeile's, of which I enclose a rather long notice, is not in anything new he has to say on the interpretation of the evangelist ; it is in his own state of mind, and in the fact that a man whose attitude to the Gospels is what his unquestionably is should be examining chaplain to Gore. A family of six children in Greenock were playing last week with a cartridge one of them had found, when it suddenly exploded, and blew off their fingers, and bits of their faces, etc., etc. ; this seems to me a parable of what will certainly happen to those people who are so sure of the Church and the Sacraments and the priesthood——'those who drank,' says McNeile of the Last Supper, ' were all priests '—and who otherwise treat the Gospels as Loisy or Schmiedel. The difficulties of Modernism, of course, are not theirs only, but they are peculiarly theirs, and they seem peculiarly unconscious of them. It does not seem to cross McNeile's mind for a moment that the very same method of study which is fatal to a certain view of the worth of the Gospels is much more immediately and unquestionably fatal to his view of the doctrinal tradition of the Church.

You must have had a very trying time lately in the political field. As far as one can judge, we must be content for a while now if we meet with no disaster, and hope that we are preparing for victory. But what a nightmare the miners' strike is. And what a fiasco even national registration might prove if passive resistance on the scale of the strike were all that was needed to defeat it. But I am persuaded better things of the nation, in spite of all the selfishness that has reigned so widely and so long, and am glad you think that on the whole things are better.

15 Lilybank Gardens, Glasgow, W.,
*September* 19, 1915.

The two volumes of Clark's International Theological Library which you sent me some time ago are disappointing additions to that series. I should have sent you a notice of them earlier if I had been able to compel myself to read them. They are in no sense books, and can only be used through the index, which is very good in the missionary one, but very inadequate in the other.

What a frightful week this has been politically. I was inclined to discount Lloyd George a little, his native and poetic temperament making his speech perhaps more telling than he knew ; but I frankly confess that Churchill startled me. The tale of failure all round was worse than I had imagined. But Churchill also has a temperament, and I believe people in large numbers just pin their faith to Kitchener and Joffre and the nature of things, and don't believe that all Europe can be overrun by the wild beasts of Berlin. I fancy the Germans know quite well all that the Government does not tell us, and the one thing which commands my unequivocal sympathy in the confusion is the demand for fuller information. Things that are not told will always be thought of outside as things too bad to tell, or things that it is some one's interest to hide. You may think it queer, but Balfour is one of the people in whom I have faith in the present crisis, and I would give a great deal to know what he really thinks about it. It is conceivable that the state of war should become chronic as well as universal, and that we should see in the twentieth century a thirty years' war as ruinous as that in the seventeenth? I am sure there is obstinacy enough for it all round if nature supplied the other conditions.

15 LILYBANK GARDENS, GLASGOW, W.,<br>
October 1, 1915.

I like Balfour's lectures [1] very much, though they leave many questions unanswered and have too many digressions. He did himself no justice when he delivered them here, and any other person who treated the public as he did would have been left with a very small audience. I cannot think very well what effect they will produce on naturalistic philosophers, but I am sure idealists will pooh-pooh them as beside the mark. The sentences I quote at the end from Höffding are remarkable parallels to much in Balfour, but Höffding, who calls his system ' critical monism,' and who raises many questions Balfour never looks at, really occupies a quite different, and, as far as

---

[1] *Theism and Humanism*, Gifford Lectures, by the Right Hon. A. J. Balfour, M.P.

I can judge, a much less Christian position. I hope Balfour's book will sell well in spite of the war, for it can do nothing but good.

It is a great pleasure to me to have Moffatt near at hand : I seem to have more interests in common with him than with any of my other colleagues. But perhaps all of us feel that with him, his interests are so various compared with those of any of us. I heard him lecture last night to the Office-Bearers' Union—excellent, and only a little impalpable for those to whom some of the ideas were unfamiliar. I am rather sorry he is preaching twice every Sunday till April, and hope he may stand it out : he is very thin.

The victory in France is evidently costing Scotland dear, but every one has been encouraged by it. I hope you have good news from your son-in-law : what a protracted trial it has been for his wife, and for you all.

15 LILYBANK GARDENS, GLASGOW, W.,
*November* 28, 1915.

I am sending with this a notice of Mr. Allan's book.[1] I hardly know him at all, and only heard my people, who are still in Greenock, speak appreciatively of him as a minister ; but

[1] *The Beautiful Thing that has happened to our Boys: Messages in War Time*, by Charles Allan, M.A.

I had read his book before you sent it, and think it is every way admirable. His taste is not exactly mine in the matter of quotations, though most that he makes are felicitous ; and he does not, like many preachers, obtrude the idea, when he quotes, of a new patch on an old garment. I hope his book will do well, for I am sure it will do good wherever it goes.

The new scale on which the war is being conducted seems to me to have the double effect of making people feel more anxious about it, and more sensible that *they* cannot manage it, and that it must be left to the management of those who are officially responsible. I think we have learned pretty well with what a discount official statements of successes have to be read, and how to discern between the lines when reverses are being coloured or disguised ; but as far as I can gather here, there is willingness to admit that fallible beings will fail somewhere, and no willingness to admit that those who are loudest in censuring their failures would never have failed themselves. Bonar Law's success in Asquith's absence has naturally been popular in Glasgow ; in Bagehot's sense of the term he is a very ' representative man,' and will in all probability have a far stronger position when the Coalition is dissolved than he ever had before. I hope in spite of the war your new books may do well.

15 Lilybank Gardens, Glasgow, W.,
*February* 7, 1916.

I ought to have sent you this notice of Mozley [1] some time ago, but though you are not giving much space to reviews I hope you can get a corner for it.  He has the courage to react against the pretentious oracular style of thing with which Westcott and Moberly hypnotised so many Anglicans, and he is not imposed on by the Broad Church people like **J. M.** Wilson, who have never discovered what the Atonement is about, and would have written the New Testament quite differently; and I think his book is likely to be useful to students and to do good in the Church.  Anyhow, it reveals a good man.

Do you think anybody knows at present how the war is going, or that anybody on our side has any grasp or control of it ?  The outside mortal opens his paper daily, and it is the same yesterday and to-day and to-morrow : never anything decisive, and too often something that has to be explained away.  The plan of waiting and nibbling *may* be the correct one, but it becomes very trying to patience when there is no unimpeachable evidence that the enemy is suffering from attrition more than we, and to the outside citizen there is at present none.  It is beginning to be felt as a humiliation that so far

---

[1] *The Doctrine of the Atonement,* by J. K. Mozley, M.A.

there has been no initiative on our side ; we have uniformly allowed the Germans to do something or to try something, and then attempted to frustrate their efforts, but all the originality seems to be with them. And all the success on land too ; for as the truth about Loos is more clearly understood, it begins to appear as the most tremendous failure in our military history. I preach every Sunday just now in a different church, and in every one there is a list of deaths and casualties. There is no weakening of resolution, but a growing impatience to see our side beginning to win. Since the Marne, a year past in September, we have piled up losses and won *nothing*. Are the Government too old ?

15 Lilybank Gardens, Glasgow, W.,
*October* 7, 1916.

You might write a Claudius Clear letter on some things connected with autobiography. Like you I have read Pepys twice, though not in twelve months, and think it in the strict sense of the term the most interesting book I know. There is not a square inch of it that has not interest, and it is as much a miracle in its way as *Othello*. A man talking to himself is interesting; a man talking to God, like Augustine in his Confessions, is interesting ; a man talking about himself, like Bunyan in *Grace*

*Abounding,* but not thinking about himself, is interesting; but a man both talking about himself and thinking about himself, like ——, bores me horribly.

We begin our classes on Thursday, but, as far as I can see, will have no first year. Only one man sat the entrance examination. Yesterday I had three Americans calling, anxious to know about climate, Zeppelins, board, etc., before they determined whether they would take a session here, in Edinburgh, or in Cambridge.

15 LILYBANK GARDENS, GLASGOW, W.,<br>
*December* 16, 1916.

I am sending you the enclosed at the request of Forrest. He is disappointed that so little notice has been taken of MacEwen, especially perhaps by old Free Church people, and he was particularly annoyed that when I spoke of him in our Presbytery on the lines of the enclosed, the *Herald* cut down its report of the Presbytery so severely that MacEwen was not even mentioned. I feel myself that it is rather belated, and that the *British Weekly* has not ignored him; but if you could get it into the Scottish part next week—in the report of our Presbytery to which there is sure to be some reference—it would please my warm-hearted colleague, to whom I have become much attached.

R

When one thinks of the political and military events of the last fortnight, it is easy to understand that the public interest will not easily be diverted to news of this kind.

I hope, now that he is in the highest place, Lloyd George will have the physique as well as the rarer qualities it demands. Ever since he had that long break over his voice, it has been easy to have misgivings about his strength ; and though the strain of the last months and years must have been tremendous, I must say I felt anxious when I heard of his beginning his new task, and such a task, with an illness. As far as I can hear, he seems to have universal good-will ; and if it was inevitable to dispense with Asquith, it is obvious on reflection that there was no way of dispensing with him that would not hurt his feelings. A widely diffused feeling that everybody in the country was more deeply concerned about the war than the Government was the real power which upset the Asquith Cabinet, and any Government which leads can count on support. I hope you are keeping up to the mark yourself. I have had an unusual amount of Central Fund meetings and correspondence, and am thankful the holidays are at hand to get a few clear days to bestow on my Cunningham Lectures.

15 LILYBANK GARDENS, GLASGOW, W.,
*December 25, 1916.*

I am doubly obliged to you for printing what I said about MacEwen—it pleased his wife and sister as well as Forrest—and for giving space to the Central Fund. Yesterday was the day when most of the churches were specially contributing to it, but of course there is no knowledge yet of how it has gone. I am hopeful, but prepared to be disappointed; I suppose you know that unbelieving frame of mind. There is a great deal of sympathy, especially among better-off people, and, after all one's pains, an immense amount of unintelligence, indifference, and suspicion : but on the whole, I expect we shall sensibly improve. I know of two ministers, both United Presbyterians, one of whom gave £30 and the other £50, but it does not seem to make the least impression on their congregations. An active conscience about such things is comparatively rare.

We had our hopes raised here about Prohibition lately, but I see the Board of Control have issued a new set of their imbecile regulations about the hours during which the public-houses may be opened, and between that and the proroguing of Parliament till February 7, it looks as if it might be long enough ere anything was done. Personally I am quite convinced that if we cannot get a Government with the moral courage to suppress this evil in spite of the Amalgamated Society of Engineers, or those who claim to speak for them, we cannot get a Government which will win the war. The present policy is a deliberate nursing of inefficiency, and if anybody says that inefficiency is negligible he is a paid liar. I don't want anything from the Control Board, but a Government with the sense and the courage to say, 'This must stop.' And it is not stopping here—nothing like it.

15 LILYBANK GARDENS, GLASGOW, W.,
*January* 14, 1917.

This is a thing about which I feel very strongly, and I have written as I feel. The lapse of the *Spectator* and the *Westminster* fills me with dismay, and I am truly glad you are sticking to your guns. The need for prohibition is as urgent as ever, and the futility of everything but prohibition was demonstrated again, if any demonstration was needed, by the incredible scenes in one of the best streets in Glasgow at the New Year—long queues of women blocking the street to get access to a public-house in which whisky was said to be sold a little cheaper than elsewhere, and that, too, day after day. It sickens me to think of it, and the only thing I can imagine more contemptible is the Pharisaic imbecility which thinks that State purchase would cure it. But this is the Sabbath day, and though I believe I do well to be angry, I don't want to curse and swear.

You are a little hard, I think, on the Churches for doing nothing ; at least I know a good many ministers who are doing what they can. I am going to a prohibition meeting at Kilmarnock on Friday, and to another in Bearsden next Wednesday, and whatever the Government may know or be ignorant of, there is no doubt that Scotland is united and sound on the question.

George Smith is staying with me to-night : I should have gone to hear him preach, but had no other time to do the article. He looks well and in good spirits.

15 LILYBANK GARDENS, GLASGOW, W.,
*January 25, 1917.*

I was truly sorry to hear you had been so long ill, and so seriously. I hope your stay at Bournemouth will do you good. The winter has been terribly long and dreary here—not so very cold but extraordinarily and persistently wet—and I have not been out of Glasgow since the first week of September either. I like your idea that when you give me a fort-night's notice I have a fortnight in which to write an article : but I will do something all the same. Perhaps not on Temperance this time :

Lord Devonport, after a lot of trifling, has hit the
nail on the head in grasping the idea that it is a
case of Bread *versus* Beer, and though he has not
driven it in to the head, he may live to be obliged
to do so.   I have an impression the Government
are getting scared about the dimensions of purchase as they go past generalities and face the
details, and I do not think it would take much
to intimidate them out of it entirely—though the
granting of prohibition is another matter.   But
the indirect intention of prohibition on the line
entered on by the Food Controller has advantages
of its own, even compared with a direct shutting
of the shops, and I am inclined to hope for most
from it.   It is just treating the publican trade
as every other unnecessary—we don't even need
to say pernicious—trade is treated.

GARELOCHHEAD,
*March* 25, 1917.

I am sorry it is only now possible for me
to acknowledge your kind letter of the 3rd.
We came here on Thursday, and I am counting on the open air, which I had not breathed
for seven weeks or so, to set me up again.
I don't know what was wrong with me : I
just collapsed suddenly and completely like
the one-hoss shay in O. W. Holmes, and I have
spent all these weeks in painfully gathering

myself in bits out of the *débris*. I am past the point of despair now, but when I shall be able to do any kind of work with body or brain I cannot foresee. I have been a little astonished at the people who condoled with me on having to postpone the Cunningham Lectures. The things I *am* sore at being unable to help at are the Temperance Cause and the Central Fund.

# INDEX

Printed in Great Britain by T. and A. CONSTABLE, Printers to His Majesty at the Edinburgh University Press

**Date Due**